*"This is a poignant look at one man's journey to his Big Why and the possibility of creating a life worth living by embracing the higher purpose in business."*

**Mo Anderson**
Vice Chairman of the Board
Keller Williams Realty

# Praise for *The Freedom Challenge*

"Here is a great example of when a true expert shares their knowledge. This book takes a seemingly difficult system, breaks it down step by step, using an entertaining and memorable story, and makes it so simple anyone could do it."

Sean Moudry
*Keller Williams Team Leader, Denver, CO*

"This is a must read for every Realtor. It took me years to develop systems and models like the ones so clearly outlined in this book. I wish I could go back and start my real estate career standing on the shoulders of these powerful principles! They are rules every top producer must live by and, therefore, thrive by."

Wayne L. Salmans
*Realtor Magazine 30 Under 30, Mat-Su Valley, AK*

"Finally! Chris Angell speaks right to the heart of an agent's real life challenges. I couldn't put this book down and forgot that I wasn't the main character in the story. After grabbing my attention, he provided proven solutions for taking control of one's business in a way that any reader could absorb. It is a quick, yet substantial read. You'll find this book to be unique, inspiring, and practical."

Don Arnold
*Former KW Team Leader & MAPS Coach, Keller, TX*

"The Freedom Challenge is a gift to share with any entrepreneur who has the talents to be successful, and is open to learning simple, strategic concepts to build a business that complements life, instead of consumes life."

Dee Dee Trosclair
*Keller Williams Regional Director, Dallas, TX*

BD —

You've been a great friend.

You are building great momentum
and a strong Brand — Keep
using Leveraged Principles.

See you at the top!

A powerful **real estate parable** that
enlightens and inspires

# The
# FREEDOM
## CHALLENGE

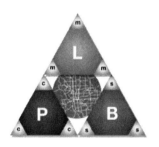

CHRIS ANGELL & CHRIS INVERSO

Published by think Media in the USA.

*The Freedom Challenge* may be purchased in bulk for educational,
business, fund-raising or sales promotional use. For information
please visit www.freedomchallengebook.com

### Publisher Cataloging-in-Publication Data

Angell, Chris.
  The freedom challenge / Chris Angell and Chris Inverso.
      p. cm.
    ISBN-13: 978-0-6155-0094-2
    1. Residential real estate—United States. 2. Success in business. I.
Inverso, Chris. II. Title.

PRINTED IN THE UNITED STATES OF AMERICA

# Acknowledgments

I'd like to say thank you to my writing partner Chris Inverso. For your tireless efforts and revisions to capture the voice and life of real estate agents everywhere. You are a gifted writer, hard worker and friend.

To Mo Anderson, thank you for your support and for championing the Higher Purpose of Business. It's not about the money…. It's about what the money can do.

To Gary Keller, thank you for creating a company that has taught me how to follow my passion, use my strengths and create a business worth owning and a life worth living.

To the agents at KW Spokane, thank you for allowing me to lead you and find new ways to strategize with you. And to Bruce Hardie for giving me the opportunity to run that business for over 4 years.

To Holly Perry, thank you for encouraging me and helping me get this started all that time ago and always carrying that first chapter I gave you in your planner.

To Josh Frost, thank you for helping me polish the images of the Freedom Formula into pictures that are easy to understand and look like more than chicken scratches on a napkin.

To Kevin Carroll, though I've never met you, your talk at Family Reunion about Play helped me think differently about my work. Sometimes the play can actually be the work.

To Michael Port, who I've also never met… your book, Book Yourself Solid, and your coaching program encouraged me to write a book to share my message.

To Bev Steiner, Mo Anderson, Dee Dee Trosclair, Sean Moudry, Don Arnold, Josh Bath, Antoinette Perez, Claudia Restrepo, Cody Gibson, Wayne Salmans, Theresa Bastian, and Erick Harpole who read the manuscript and gave me their feedback.

To Rob Henry, Bo Apele, Bryan Avante, Tara Hayden, Denise Ashcroft thank you for standing in my corner and encouraging my every step.

To my Mom, thank you for always giving me room to learn and live as I go. You are my hero and role model of what it means to be a parent. I would not take on life the way I do if you hadn't raised me the way you did.

Finally, and mostly, thank you to my amazing wife and kids. You have given me the foundation to pursue and chase my Higher Purpose of Business, constantly encouraging me, high-fiving me and telling me how much you believe in me.  I love you forever.

*- Chris Angell*

# Acknowledgments

I would like to thank my coauthor Chris Angell for giving me the opportunity to work on this project and for providing the powerful content and formulas. Your patience and vision know no bounds and my respect for you is great. I am honored to call you a friend.

To my loving parents, John and Marlene Inverso, I couldn't have asked for a more loving and supportive home to grow up in. Mom, thank you for seeing my potential and for mentoring me as a writer. Dad, your belief in me means more than you know.

To Forrest "Frosty" Westering, playing football for you at PLU was a life changing experience. Every day I am reminded of the life lessons that you taught me and I am a better husband, father, and friend because of them. Ding How!

To my fellow EMAL football players, your pursuit of excellence in life inspires me to pursue excellence myself.

To Mike Hodson and Jerrod Sessler, thank you for the great friends and mentors you've both been to me over the years.

To Patrick Lencioni, Bob Burg, John David Mann, Ken Blanchard, Sheldon Bowles, Spencer Johnson, Todd Hopkins, Ray Hilbert, and Bruce Wilkinson, each of your parable like fictional works inspired my writing. I truly stand on your shoulders.

To Diane Morton, who provided early editing support and expressed great enthusiasm about the early manuscript, you are a great friend and a continual encouragement to me.

With all my heart I want to thank my wife, Tharen, and daughters Siri, Elise, and Macy. You each have given up so much so that I could follow my dreams. In the years that come my desire is to do the same for you. I love you to the moon and back.

- *Chris Inverso*

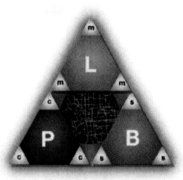

# CONTENTS

*Foreword*                                          1

*Chapter One –* A Challenging Day                   3

*Chapter Two –* Hollow Victory                      23

*Chapter Three –* The Meeting                       38

*Chapter Four –* The Freedom Formula                50

*Chapter Five –* It All Starts with Focus           69

*Chapter Six –* The People Principle                77

*Chapter Seven –* The Brand Principle               92

*Chapter Eight –* The Leverage Principle            117

*Chapter Nine –* Playing the Game                   140

*Chapter Ten –* Living It Out                       165

*Authors' Note to Reader*                           175

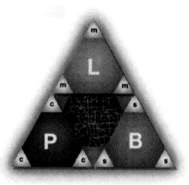

# FOREWORD

There aren't many industries that have the flexibility and income potential as real estate. This could be the perfect business for people to fund the life of their dreams. However, as a CEO, coach, trainer and agent myself, I've seen the hurdles agents face trying to build a strong, sustainable and scalable business model that pays them even when they don't want to work anymore.

I believe that business should fund your dreams and create the life you want. Everyone has a Higher Purpose when their needs are met and they have their fill of toys. The trick, once you have the money, is to find the time. In the Freedom Challenge I outline a model that not only allows you to build a business that funds your life but also gives you the time to enjoy it. Everyone's dreams or

Higher Purpose, when lived out, make a difference for others. Your business should help you fund that difference.

As you read these pages, please think about your own Higher Purpose, your goals and dreams, and consider whether or not you're willing to accept The Freedom Challenge.

Your Dreams Matter.

*- Chris Angell*

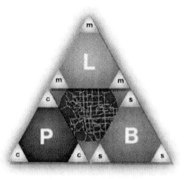

# CHAPTER ONE

Chuck closed his eyes and exhaled deeply in an attempt to quiet his frustration. He'd never cared much for 'on hold' music and on a day like today he wasn't sure if he could take much more of it. Overall, he considered himself a reasonably patient person, but he couldn't stand it when people, or things, wasted his time.

Today wasn't just any day. It was a Friday. Not only was it a Friday, but there were only two more banking days left in the month. And, he had three transactions yet to close.

This was also the day of his daughter Rachael's big violin recital which was scheduled at 4:15 pm. Like most events of this nature, it was to be followed by a celebration dinner at 7 pm.

Chuck glanced at his watch. So much had already happened today and it was only 10:30 am. To make matters worse, his part time assistant Amy was on the first week of her three week honeymoon. This meant that Chuck was flying solo.

Just before the title company's jingle restarted for the fourth time, the sound of a hurried female voice finally registered in Chuck's ears, "Really sorry to keeping you waiting, it's been one of those mornings."

"Tell me about it Lisa," Chuck replied. "I know where we are on the Barkley and Kappert closings, but what about Geiger?"

Lisa rustled through the paper work on her desk for a moment. "We're waiting on loan documents and I haven't heard back from the lender. At this point even if they got me docs, I'm not going to have time to work this file up and get them in to sign today," she said.

Chuck wasn't one to give up easily, "Hey Lisa, I know you have a lot on your plate, but I really need to get Geiger in today. If I can make sure you get the documents by noon, can you make it happen? I'm not looking for a miracle here, just a life boat so I can get to shore."

"I'll see what I can do, but I'm not making any

promises," Lisa replied hesitantly.

Chuck then decided to press a little harder, "So, what if I don't get them to you until 1:00 pm?"

"Don't push it mister. Listen, I really got to run. Good luck!" And, with the click of the phone, Lisa was gone.

Chuck didn't allow the receiver to return to the cradle before he hurriedly dialed another number.

As soon as the other party answered Chuck set the tone for the conversation, "Mark, the loan documents for Geiger were supposed to be out yesterday. What's going on?"

"Gee Chuck, I'm not sure. Let me check with underwriting and I'll call you right back," Mark replied.

Little did Chuck know it, but this would be the last time he would speak with Mark until much later that afternoon. However, there was no time to sit around and worry. Outside of the two voicemail messages he would eventually leave for Mark, Chuck found himself knee deep in other issues.

Earlier that morning, when Chuck had first unlocked the door to his office, he had been greeted by several faxes. One of which was an inspection response from the potential buyers of one of his 17 active listings.

As he scanned the document, he shook his head in disgust and muttered the words, "Rookie agent." State law required that he present this response to his sellers, but he already knew that they would reject it.

Once the formality of corresponding with his sellers was out of the way, he had placed a call to Jesse, the agent for the buyers. Chuck wasn't surprised that he had to leave Jesse a message. It was just after 8:30 am and Chuck was willing to bet he wasn't even awake yet.

He tried not to let himself be bothered by Jesse, but he didn't have much patience for undisciplined and unprofessional agents. In his own words, "All they do is waste my time and give the real agents out there a bad name."

When Jesse called back later that morning, Chuck was ready for him. "Jesse, I'm looking at the inspection response form right now and I don't know what to say. It looks like you expect my sellers to build your buyers a whole new house?"

Jesse knew Chuck by reputation only and wasn't sure what to say. He'd made a lot of promises to his buyers, but in his gut he knew they'd asked for too much. The truth was that he had only sold a handful of homes and Jesse realized that he was likely outmatched by Chuck.

Still, he wasn't going to make this easy.

"Chuck, have you been through this house? It needs a lot of work," Jesse responded as nonchalantly as he could. Before Chuck could reply, Jesse followed his comment up with a soft threat, "And, there are a lot of other houses out there that my buyers could be looking at."

Chuck had been in enough of these situations to know how to handle himself. A high percentage of the time he could just power through these negotiations by using nothing other than his strong personality.

However, experience had also taught him that with a pinch of friendly finesse he could improve his odds even more. The trick was letting the other agent save a little face.

In the most pleasant tone he could muster Chuck said "Listen, Jesse, maybe we got off on the wrong foot. I'm impressed by the way you've represented your buyers. You've put together a strong offer and they've got a lot to thank you for."

Chuck paused for dramatic effect, "The way I see it, we just need to work out a few small details and we can get this deal done."

There was silence on the other end of the phone, but

Chuck swore he could hear Jesse's chest puffing up with new found pride. He knew his words were working. Chuck had built him up and now he was going to tear him down.

"Jesse, I'll be honest with you. These sellers of mine are grizzly bears and I mean the man-eating kind. They're the real deal and they are not going to back down."

Just as quickly as the air entered Jesse's chest, it rushed back out. Chuck had him right where he wanted him.

Chuck now spoke slowly, but confidently, "However, I do see how this can work. I think there are a couple items that might be negotiable and I'll see what I can do with my sellers. If I can get these concessions for you, then I'll let you bring them back to your buyers and tell them that you personally beat me down."

In truth, Chuck had already spoken with his sellers and they had already given him a short list of token items to which they would commit.

"Now, how does that sound?" Chuck softly asked Jesse.

Jesse felt like he'd just been on a roller coaster. He'd intended to put up more of a fight, but he decided to cash out while he was still ahead. "Gosh, that sounds great Chuck!" he responded enthusiastically.

With that phone call over with, Chuck wondered why everything wasn't this easy. Then he looked at his watch, groaned, and retracted his last thought. Nothing was easy. It was 2:45 pm and there was a long list of items that he still had to address. How did he ever think he'd be able to survive without his assistant Amy?

He had a new listing appointment at 3:00 pm, he still hadn't heard back from Mark on the Geiger file, another client, Mr. Malkamus, was threatening to cancel his existing listing, and he had to return numerous other phone calls. Even if he left now, he was going to be late for the 3:00 pm listing appointment.

As Chuck hurriedly gathered his things, he formed a quick plan in his head. Mr. Malkamus was retired and always home, so he'd swing by and see him after he secured the new listing.

"I am going to get the new listing," he told himself.

Finally, he'd make most of his phone calls while he was driving and, if everything went well, he'd have just enough time to get to the recital by 4:15 pm.

For every listing appointment, Chuck made it a habit of inspecting the entire block before arriving no later than ten minutes early. However, there was no time for such an investigation today. As it was, Chuck pulled up to the house at three minutes past the hour, which meant, by his book, he was thirteen minutes late.

After knocking on the potential client's door for the second time Chuck noticed that there were no cars in the driveway. Removing his phone from the holster on his hip, he dialed the number he had written on his prospect information sheet.

Chuck held the phone to his ear, listened to what felt to be an abnormally long sequence of rings, and, when prompted, left a polite and professional message. He commented on the fine condition of the home, conveyed his enthusiasm for getting the house sold, and relayed that he would wait for them in his car until 3:15 pm.

Back inside the comfort of his foreign luxury sedan, Chuck began to move methodically through his list of phone calls. When he finally looked as his watch it was 3:25 pm. Not only was he running behind, but he had been stood up!

Few things bothered Chuck more than a no-show client. He had worked hard to break free from the unprofessional image that most people associate with real estate agents. This meant that he always did what he said he would do, always arrived when he said he was going to arrive, and always called in advance of his commitments if he needed to make a change. In return, he expected the same from everyone he worked with, including his clients.

With steam rising from his forehead, Chuck started his vehicle, put it in gear, and drove toward the residence of John Malkamus, his unhappy seller. He was actually making good time until a school bus pulled onto the road ahead of him. For the next few miles, the flashing red lights on the back of the bus taunted him each time he was forced to stop behind it.

When Chuck finally pulled up to his destination he could see Mr. Malkamus watering his roses on the side of his home. Before he exited the vehicle he took a quick moment to refocus himself. He emerged with a sense of confidence that was backed by the fierce determination that had made him who he was.

"Good afternoon, Mr. Malkamus," said Chuck as he lifted his sunglasses and smiled to greet the elderly gentleman standing in front of him.

"Is it?" said Mr. Malkamus as he looked sideways at Chuck. "Why is it that I can't get your attention unless I threaten to cancel my listing?"

With that Mr. Malkamus turned back to his roses and resumed his watering.

Chuck was not shaken. He was prepared for a less than enthusiastic reception and had already rehearsed an apology that he hoped would appease his troubled client.

"I'm very sorry Mr. Malkamus, I did receive your messages, but I've been very busy. My assistant is on vacation, and I'm doing the best I can without her."

"Are you?" Mr. Malkamus' tone indicated that he wasn't convinced. "Look, I know that I'm selling a small older rambler and that you have many clients with much nicer houses. I don't expect to be treated just like everyone else, but I do expect my phone calls to be returned."

"I can appreciate that, Mr. Malkamus. At the moment you have my undivided attention. Now what can I do for you?" replied Chuck with as much patience he could muster.

"Do you know what kind of roses these are?" Mr. Malkamus asked.

"I'm sorry?" responded Chuck.

"Do you know what kind of roses these are?" Mr. Malkamus repeated himself.

"No, I'm afraid I don't," Chuck finally admitted as he

wondered what the roses had to do with anything.

Mr. Malkamus gestured with his left hand while he spoke in an informative tone. "These here are Bourbon roses, over there I have two varieties of Damask roses, and those on the far side are my prized Noisette roses." When he was done, he turned for the first time to face Chuck and caught Chuck checking his watch.

"You still don't get it, do you?" Mr. Malkamus asked.

Chuck did his best to mask his embarrassment for getting caught and his overall growing impatience. With a forced smile and measured words he attempted to move their conversation forward.

"Mr. Malkamus, your roses are exceptionally beautiful and I can see that you are very proud of them. However, my commitment to you is to get your home sold as quickly as possible for top dollar. I know that you are unhappy about something, and I came here today to figure out what it is."

Mr. Malkamus nodded silently, turned to his roses, and resumed his watering yet one more time. He seemed saddened as he spoke.

"Chuck, almost anyone can go down to one of those 'big box' hardware stores or to a nursery, buy a rose bush or two, come home, and drop them in the ground. What they cannot do is buy roses like mine. Why? Because these are old world roses from the nineteenth century that have been in the ground for more than one hundred years. Conservatively, I'd say the value of my rose garden is somewhere between $5,000 and $10,000."

With that, Mr. Malkamus turned back to Chuck. "The reason I've been leaving you messages is that, when I listed my house with you, you said that you'd include my roses in the listing description. Well, last weekend my daughter helped me get on the internet, or whatever it is that you call it, and look at my listing on the computer. My point is, the description doesn't say anything about my roses and I'd like you to change that."

Chuck was now officially upset. Still, he maintained his professionalism. He did remember discussing the roses when he took the listing but he'd been in a hurry at the time and the roses didn't seem that important. Why hadn't Mr. Malkamus just said what he wanted in the messages?

"So, you don't really want to cancel your listing?" Chuck asked.

"No, but I wanted to send you a message. You see, I listed my house with you because I knew you were good at what you do. At the same time, I've always felt like a number to you and that bothers me. Sure, you smile and say all the right things, but you're always so busy. Sometimes you really do need to stop, smell the roses, and treat people for who they are, not what they can do for you."

Inside Chuck was still boiling, but he turned on his graceful charm and offered the best confession he could.

"You're right Mr. Malkamus. I shouldn't rush the important things in life. I promise that I'll do better and I'll add your roses to the description. Is there anything else I can do while I'm here?"

"Yes, take these to your wife," said Mr. Malkamus as he clipped several large, beautiful roses, wrapped them carefully, and handed them to Chuck.

Mr. Malkamus continued, "With your busy schedule you probably haven't brought her any of these in a while." Then he paused. "You are married aren't you?" he asked.

Chuck nodded but he wasn't sure if he was admitting to being married or the fact that he hadn't brought home flowers recently. Both were true.

Back inside his car, Chuck raced to the recital. It was now 3:55 pm and if he timed things right, he'd only be fifteen minutes late. It would likely earn him a disapproving look from his wife, but nothing more. Besides, Rachael, his daughter, was the second recitalist so he wouldn't miss a minute of her performance.

As he drove, his thoughts drifted back to Mr. Malkamus. The guy had some nerve to threaten to cancel his listing and waste Chuck's time just because he wanted to teach him a ridiculous lesson. Chuck had several lessons he'd like to teach Mr. Malkamus himself.

What did he expect from Chuck anyway? Chuck was good at what he did, he worked hard, and, most importantly, he delivered results. Mr. Malkamus should have just told him what he wanted and he would have taken care of it. What a crazy old man!

Still, Mr. Malkamus' words reverberated inside his head. He could still hear Mr. Malkamus saying, "Do you know what kind of roses these are…I always felt like a number to you….you probably haven't brought her any of these in a while…"

Chuck shook his head. There just wasn't enough time in a day. He pursed his lips and vowed to work harder and longer.

As he pulled up to a stoplight, Chuck felt his phone vibrate. He looked down to see a text message from his wife. Before he could respond, an incoming call from

Mark flashed across the screen.

Mark began talking as soon as Chuck accepted the call. "Chuck I'm sorry to be calling you so late in the day, but I'm glad I caught you. I finally got to the bottom of the Geiger file, and I only need two things."

Chuck didn't like the sound of this. "What are we looking at Mark?" he asked with an edge in his voice.

"Well, I need a legible copy of page 22 of the purchase contract and there is also a letter of explanation that I need to have Mr. and Mrs. Geiger sign," Mark answered.

"Can't these be prior to funding conditions? When do you need them?" Chuck asked.

"You see, that's the thing, I need to get these tonight. They want them prior to docs, but I've got an underwriter who is willing to stay late to prep everything so the Geigers can sign first thing Monday morning," Mark responded.

"You've got to be kidding me, Mark," Chuck practically yelled. "Since I hadn't heard from you, I assumed that you'd gotten the documents to Lisa and that the Geigers had already signed. We need to close on Monday, not sign on Monday. Now you're telling me they haven't even signed yet. The last day to close is

Tuesday and you know that I can't stand to leave things until the last minute."

"I know and I'm sorry," Mark stated. "I called in a big favor tonight to get this done, but I still need your help."

Chuck couldn't believe it. His wife, Glori, was going to skewer and roast him alive. Even worse, he could already see the disappointment on Rachael's face, when he showed up late for her recital. He pounded his steering wheel in frustration.

"Alright, spell it out for me. Tell me exactly what needs to happen," Chuck demanded with venom in his voice.

"Well, I'm stuck here helping the underwriter. So, I'll email you the letter that needs to be signed. The Geigers get off work at 5:30 pm and I'll tell them to head straight to your office. Once they sign it, I'll need you to fax it to me along with your copy of page 22 of the purchase contract. We'll take care of everything else on our end."

The light was still red when their call ended and Chuck quickly typed an obligatory message to his wife. It read, "Work related emergency…will meet you at dinner."

When he got back to his office, Chuck made good use of

his time by sending Jesse the updated inspection response form with the list of 'negotiated' repairs to which his sellers had agreed. Chuck smiled as he fed the paper in the fax machine. "At least this situation had been easy," he said to himself.

While he was still waiting for the Geigers to arrive, he prepped some of his files and prospecting lists for the upcoming week. Even when Amy was around, this was still part of his weekly routine. She was great at helping him out with basic things, but for some reason he couldn't get her to think like him when it came to things like this.

"That's what I really need," he thought, "Another Chuck. In fact, make that two."

Chuck became so engrossed in his work that he forgot about the time. It was nearly 6:30 pm when he finally heard a knock on his office door. He opened it to find the Geigers standing in front of him.

"We came as soon as we could," Mr. Geiger apologized. "Marcy had car trouble so I had to pick her up."

Despite the pressure he was under, Chuck knew better than to chastise them. He could still make it to dinner if he hurried. With the wave of his hand he graciously invited them in. "This should only take a minute," he affirmed.

Chuck was right. The signing took exactly one minute. However, the Geigers had a lot of questions. He did the best he could to answer all of them, even the ones he had answered previously.

It was 7:15 pm when he finally escorted them to the front door of his building and returned to pack his things. After he retrieved a confirmation that his fax to Mark had been sent, he turned to shut down his desktop computer. Before he could do so, he heard someone call for him down the hallway.

"Chuck? What are you still doing here?" a familiar voice asked.

"I'm asking myself the same question," Chuck said dryly. "How are you, Bev?"

"Fine, thank you. Hey, I actually wanted to talk with you. I was looking at one of your listings online today and the virtual tour link wasn't working. I tried it multiple times. I also looked at several of your other listings and I had the same problem. I think something may be wrong with your entire virtual tour library."

"Great, that's exactly what I need," Chuck replied sarcastically without any attempt to hide his frustration.

He was almost too tired to care, but he forced himself to send his virtual tour sales rep a brief email regarding the situation before he turned his computer off.

Bev continued to talk while Chuck typed, "Well, I don't feel too sorry for you. I saw your $1.6 million listing that you posted this month. How'd you do it? I'd give an arm and a leg to snag a listing like that."

For a brief moment Chuck forgot about his problems. People had been talking about his big listing all month and it was very satisfying to see that his peers were genuinely impressed by his achievement. Truth be told, Chuck had even impressed himself. It was the biggest listing of his career.

Before anything else could go wrong, Chuck shut down his computer, thanked Bev for her help, and locked his office for the night.

There was no reason to hurry at this point. The damage had been done. He'd missed the recital and the dinner. As he walked to his car, Chuck's subconscious reminded him of something he wasn't too proud of: this wasn't the first time his family had become a casualty of a work day gone bad.

Despite the fact that his family would likely still be at the restaurant, Chuck elected to head straight home. He wanted to postpone answering the inevitable string of questions that he knew Glori would ask about his afternoon and evening.

As Chuck drove he noticed the light flashing on his phone that indicated he had a voice message. He must have missed a call while he was speaking with Bev.

Using his phone's speed dial function he accessed a voicemail message from Jesse. The message said, "Hey Chuck, Jesse here. I just spoke with my buyers about the list of repair items that you faxed over tonight. I tried to follow the plan you suggested earlier today, but now my buyers are talking about pulling the plug on the whole deal. Call me."

Chuck was speechless. In a day when he needed it the most, nothing had come together. But, as frustrated and discouraged as he was, he was equally determined. Just as he had always done in the past, he would find a way to succeed. There was no alternative.

# CHAPTER TWO

'Message Sent.' Although these two words registered in Chuck's mind, he continued to stare at them with bloodshot eyes until they seemed to jump from his computer screen.

The clock on his desk read 6:42 pm and with the single click of his mouse he effectively ended what had been the most intense 48 hours of his five year real estate career. He'd never been more relieved that a month was actually over.

From beginning to end, the last two days had been filled with countless phone calls, emails, faxes, addendums, loan documents, handshakes, and more than one forced smile. Sheer willpower and eighty three ounces of fine Columbian coffee had been the secrets to his success.

And successful he had been. Chuck sat back in his chair and recounted the events of the past few days.

First was the Geiger transaction. All Chuck's efforts from the previous Friday had paid off. Early on Monday, the Geigers had signed their loan documents and all the accompanying closing paperwork.

From that moment on Chuck had monitored the transaction in the same way that a doctor monitors a patient in the ICU. Late that afternoon, he'd received the final word that everything had recorded with the county.

Somehow he'd also made time for his new friend Jesse and had successfully negotiated the inspection response. It had required a bit of a dance on his part, but he found a way to make it work for all parties involved. As long as the financing held up, this would be one of seven transactions already set to close next month.

Not only did he add Mr. Malkamus' roses to the listing description, but he hired a contract photographer to go by and capture two dozen photos of his client's garden.

From this collection, Chuck selected an additional two photographs that he added to the listing. Based on his most recent conversation with Mr. Malkamus, things couldn't be better on his end.

Bev had been right about the links to his virtual tours; they were all broken. A programming error on the part of his vendor led to a regional outage that had lasted through the weekend.

On Monday morning he dedicated some time to give his sales rep a call so he could deliver a piece of his mind. All he got in return was a less than satisfying but sincere apology and a promise that everything had been fixed.

He'd even been able to patch things up with Glori. Things were definitely icy on Friday night, but they thawed quickly on Saturday morning when Chuck woke up early and made breakfast for the entire family.

His famous apple cinnamon pancakes were always a crowd pleaser and Glori couldn't believe how beautiful the roses were that he'd brought home from Mr. Malkamus.

Perhaps the most remarkable event had been a phone call Chuck had received that very morning. It was so significant that Chuck would later refer to it as 'The Call'.

At approximately 9:07 am Chuck's mobile phone rang and displayed an unidentified number. When he answered the voice on the other end introduced herself as Janice Kraken, personal assistant to Guy Chamberlain.

"Guy Chamberlain?" Chuck asked himself in disbelief. Instantly, his body straightened in his chair and his head snapped to attention.

Using flawless diction, Chuck carried on with Janice in a highly professional sounding tone that he largely reserved for important meetings.

Chuck's end of the conversation sounded like this, "Yes, I would be willing to meet with Mr. Chamberlain ….Yes, I am available on Friday afternoon….Confirmed, 1:00 pm will work."

Despite his formal sounding response, the unexpected call had caught Chuck off guard and his mind was racing. He nearly hung up before he remembered that he hadn't asked a very important question.

"Excuse me, Janice?" he asked. Chuck wasn't sure if she was still on the line.

"Yes, Chuck?" Janice responded.

"What is the nature of my meeting with Mr. Chamberlain?" Chuck asked, recovering his composure.

"Oh, I'm not sure. He said it was a confidential business matter. Does that help?" she replied.

"Yes, I believe it does. Thank you." Chuck said.

Chuck still wasn't sure what the meeting was about, but he wanted to leave Janice with the impression that he was firmly in control of the situation and that everything was proceeding as he expected.

Guy Chamberlain was a legend in the Reed County real estate community, a near immortal. In fact, Chuck wouldn't have been surprised if Guy resided on Mt. Olympus with Zeus and the rest of the mythological Greek gods.

Almost every major commercial real estate transaction in the area had Guy's fingerprints on it. Rumor also had it that some fifteen to twenty years earlier Guy had been the king of residential real estate in Reed County as well.

Although there was no hard evidence to support this, from time to time Chuck saw a residential listing with an elegant 'For Sale' sign that bore an English coat of arms. In the back of his mind, Chuck suspected that these listings were somehow connected to Guy Chamberlain.

Overall, Chuck was conflicted. Thinking about Guy Chamberlain forced him to process thoughts and feelings that he would never share publically.

Although he hadn't reached Guy's level of success, he

believed himself to be cut from a similar cloth. To date, Chuck had out performed many of his industry peers and enjoyed a strong reputation in the marketplace.

At the same time, individuals like Guy Chamberlain reminded Chuck that there was yet a higher level of achievement, one that he had not reached.

Chuck believed that he truly belonged at that level, but today he wasn't even close. In fact, he couldn't see a clear path to get there and this made him feel strangely uncomfortable.

On one hand he clearly respected and admired Guy Chamberlain and on the other he felt a sense of rivalry and contempt that was fueled by pride. Nonetheless, he was honored by the meeting invitation and was intrigued by the idea of being an insider in a 'confidential business matter' involving Guy.

With that, Chuck's mind recoiled from his daydream. All in all it hadn't been a bad month. He'd put in a herculean effort and closed eight hard earned transactions, including the hard fought Geiger deal. All of this called for a celebration, even if it was a small one.

And small it would be. Glori was tied up with a community event that would extend well into the evening and their children were staying over at friends' houses for the night. Still, Chuck was determined to reward himself for his efforts and he knew just the place for such an indulgence.

Max's BBQ was located on the other side of town, just off the Old Mountain Highway, in a business district that had once thrived prior to the construction of the interstate freeway 40 years earlier.

At one point in time the rundown building had been home to a roadside diner. Today, a single neon sign emblazoned with the name 'Max's BBQ' bathed the parking lot in a pink glow.

Max, the proprietor of the establishment, was a fourth generation Bar-B-Que chef from Decatur, Alabama. He'd opened Max's about five years earlier and his motto was simple, "Serve the best Northern Alabama BBQ money can buy and make people smile."

The menu at Max's included many of the items one would expect from a BBQ joint: two types of pork ribs, laved on pork shoulder, beef brisket, and hand-made hot links.

However, Max was best known for his signature chicken which featured a tangy, vinegar based white sauce instead a sweet, tomato based sauce.

This sauce, known as, 'The Max', came from a well-protected family recipe and had won numerous awards at fairs and cook-offs around the country.

Tuesday nights were typically slow nights at Max's BBQ and there were only a handful of customers seated in the restaurant when Chuck walked in. There was no host, so he selected a table near the back of the dining room and settled in.

Moments later, Max burst through a door just to the right of Chuck's table. His arms were occupied with two huge trays of food. Chuck watched as Max graciously served two young couples with twice the amount of food required for a party their size.

When Max was confident that his guests had all they needed he turned to make his way back to the kitchen. After a step or two he spotted Chuck.

"Chuck, to what do I owe this unexpected pleasure," Max exclaimed as he set his empty tray on a nearby table.

"Well, let's just say it's been an interesting month and I need some TLC in the form of some comfort food," Chuck replied.

"I see," nodded Max knowingly, "the Sampler for you?"

"That's what I was hoping for," Chuck responded with a smile, "with a large sweet tea when you have a moment."

Chuck and Max met a few years earlier through the local chamber of commerce. Soon afterward, Chuck stopped in to try Max's chicken for the first time and was smitten. Not only did Chuck become a regular customer, but he also helped Max buy his house about a year later.

It wasn't long before Max slid two plates of his best BBQ in front of Chuck. On the tray he had two glasses of sweet tea instead of one.

"Mind if I join you for a bit," Max asked. He gestured over his shoulder and continued, "Everyone has what they need for the next few minutes."

"So, how's business…everything ok?" inquired Max, looking a little worried.

Chuck couldn't help but smile at his friend's genuine display of concern. He realized that his earlier comment had been misleading.

"Yes, thanks for asking, Max. Everything is ok. In fact, business is good." Chuck paused for a moment to measure his words.

"However, the last few days of this month were particularly difficult. In the end I got the outcome I wanted; it just took a lot more effort than it should have."

Chuck paused again to take a sip of tea.

"Don't get me wrong, Max. I don't have a problem with hard work. I put in a lot of hours every day and take great pride in thinking proactively about my business. Still, there are times when things just seem to get out of control."

As he spoke, Chuck felt surprised that he was sharing so deeply with Max. At the same time, he sensed that Max somehow understood what he was saying.

"At the end of a day like this, I can't help but wonder, is this as good as it gets?" Chuck continued.

"In the past, when I was able to rise above pressure situations I saw it as a clear sign that I was one of the best. Now, I'm not so sure. I'm still proud of my performance and think I'm one of the best, I just wonder if I'll always have the energy to keep this up."

Chuck's voice trailed off after his last statement and the two men sat in silence for a moment.

So far Max had done nothing but listen intently while quietly sipping his tea and nodding.

"Chuck, in many ways we live the same life." Max stated almost apologetically.

"Like you, I left the world of traditional employment five years ago. My grandfather leveraged the money he made in the restaurant business to buy up real estate in our home town. When he passed away, I inherited a modest sum and used it to follow in his footsteps," Max shared.

"The day I opened Max's BBQ felt like the most liberating day in my life," he continued. "I knew I was going to have to put in a lot of hard work, but finally I was working and earning for myself. What's more, I got to call all the shots. It was my name on the sign and my reputation that was on the line."

Chuck was busy enjoying the feast Max had prepared for him and he nodded for Max to continue.

"At first, everything was fun. I didn't mind running here and there when we ran out of this or that. Going to the bank and depositing money was exhilarating. Late nights and big crowds were simply signs that I was headed in the right direction. No matter how hectic things got, I was able to rise to the challenge. I literally felt as if I could do no wrong and it seemed as though mastery of this business was right around the corner."

This was all beginning to sound familiar to Chuck. He wiped his mouth and asked, "So, what changed?"

"That's the thing," Max replied. "I can't pinpoint the moment, but remember waking up early one morning feeling especially tired. As my body was coming to grips with the reality of a new day, a thought popped into my mind, one that I haven't been able to get rid of since that time. The thought was, 'I wonder if this is as good as it gets'."

Chuck no longer doubted Max's earlier statement about the similarity of their lives and their businesses. However, he was curious where Max's story would end, so he chose not to interrupt him.

"The more I've thought about it, the stronger the feeling has become. The success that I hoped for when I opened Max's, the success I still long for, always seems to be just beyond my grasp."

"In fact, every last minute trip to the store, every server that calls in sick, and every customer check that gets returned for insufficient funds, all seem to push real success farther and farther away."

"I don't want to mislead you. Max's has done well and I earn enough to cover my family's basic needs plus a little extra. At the same time, it's nothing like I had originally hoped," Max finished.

"You're not ready to give up are you," Chuck asked

with feigned disbelief. "This chicken is amazing and I don't know how I'd live without it."

Max smiled, waved his hand, and looked to the side in a display of mock embarrassment.

"Seriously, your chicken is that good," Chuck prodded.

Then he adopted a more serious expression, "About the business, you're not going to throw in the towel are you?"

"Absolutely not!" Max said in a friendly, but resolute tone. "I'm more determined than ever to succeed. In fact, I recently learned something from my 15 year old son that I think may help me."

"My son is taking a driver education class after school each Monday. Last week I arrived early to pick him up and slipped in the back of the classroom. As I was standing there, the instructor wrapped up the session by reading aloud from the course textbook," Max continued.

Chuck then watched as Max pulled a folded piece from the back pocket of his pants.

"The passage was so powerful I asked for a copy," Max confessed. "This is what she read,

'After narrowly missing an accident, many new drivers are tricked into believing that they have mastered driving because they were able to react quickly in an emergency. Nothing could be further from the truth. The masters of driving are those who constantly monitor the environment and perform the fundamentals of defensive driving. These drivers adjust their trajectory before accidents have a chance to happen and practically eliminate the need for evasive maneuvers altogether.'

"As soon as I heard this, I knew what I needed for my business. Chuck, I need a plan that can help me eliminate my business' need for evasive maneuvers."

"In the past, when I've run into challenges, I've just vowed to redouble my efforts and work harder. In effect, I've only been committing to get better at evasive maneuvers."

"Now I know it's time for me to work both harder and smarter. I'm just not sure what that means at a practical level," Max admitted.

Now everything had come full circle for Chuck. He and Max were suffering a similar fate, but they were not defeated. Although he would have been reluctant to admit it to Max, it was comforting to know that another top businessperson was facing the same obstacles that he was.

Chuck now realized that he what he needed to do

was to adjust his course and learn to get better at 'driving' his business, instead of getting better at evasive maneuvers. But how?

Chuck thanked Max for the hearty meal and tipped his friend generously. Before he parted, they both promised to share anything that might help the other in their mutual quest for business mastery.

As Chuck drove home, thoughts seemed to fly by him like the headlights of the oncoming cars.

This month had been a success, yet something was clearly missing.

He knew that he was good at what he did, yet he wondered if the thrill of one too many evasive maneuvers had tricked him into thinking he was better than he was.

He was determined to succeed in a bigger way, yet he wasn't sure how.

He was willing to work hard, yet he didn't want to continue to rob time from his family.

What was the next step?

Where, did he go from here?

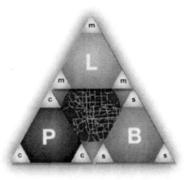

# CHAPTER **THREE**

Chuck was not easily intimidated by anyone, but he did hold a very high opinion of Guy Chamberlain. Despite this, no special preparation was required for their meeting. Professional dress was already a part of his everyday routine and he was quite skilled at interacting with individuals from all walks of life.

Overall, Chuck was optimistic about the meeting. Guy's interest in him obviously represented some kind of opportunity. He had a feeling that this opportunity, whatever it was, would help him take his business to the next level.

In reality, he had no idea what he was in for.

Chuck arrived at his destination on time, which meant he was fifteen minutes early by traditional standards. This gave him plenty of time to park and get a lay of the land.

Janice, Guy's assistant, had assured Chuck that membership at the Beaumont Golf and Country Club was not required in order to dine at the Creek Side Lounge. This was confirmed when he checked in with the maître d'. After his name was verified in the leather bound reservation book he was quickly escorted to a table set for two with a striking view of the surrounding nature preserve.

It's not that Chuck couldn't afford a membership at Beaumont, it's that he thought that he'd never have the time to enjoy it. In fact, he was truly shocked to see how many people were preparing to tee off for a round of golf this early on a workday.

Chuck scanned the room as he waited for Guy to arrive. The Creek Side Lounge was a little less than half full and most of the patrons appeared to be either middle aged or retired professionals.

His eye's finally settled on two men engaged in a lively conversation by the bar. A short, older man, who was seated, roared with laughter. A tall, well-dressed man playfully slapped the short man's back as he delivered an animated narrative.

Captivated, Chuck watched until the two men finally finished their conversation, shook hands, and offered each other parting words.

As the tall man turned to leave, Chuck instantly recognized him as none other than Guy Chamberlain. His prominent physical features were unmistakable, especially since Chuck had seen so many pictures of him over the years in news publications.

When Guy neared his table, Chuck rose to greet him. In response, Guy offered Chuck a hearty hello and a firm handshake. As he did so, he briefly rested his left hand on Chuck's right shoulder.

"Chuck," Guy said warmly, "thanks for making the time to meet with me."

"It's my pleasure," replied Chuck.

Once they took their seats, a server appeared immediately to take their order. Before Chuck could speak up, Guy began whispering into the gentleman's ear. When Guy finished the server turned and walked quickly toward the kitchen.

Guy then turned to Chuck. "Chuck, you're probably wondering why I invited you here," he stated.

Chuck nodded as Guy paused.

"A close friend of mine would like to buy the Carlton

Estate and I wanted to present her offer to you in person," Guy shared in a relaxed, conversational tone.

Chuck was floored. He was both excited and disappointed at the same time.

On one hand he was pleased to have an offer so quickly on his prized $1.6 million listing. Based on current market conditions, Chuck had anticipated that he'd have to wait at least six to nine months before the property would receive this level of interest.

On the other hand he'd hoped for something more from his meeting with Guy. Ever since Janice's call earlier in the week, Chuck had entertained visions of being part of one of the big business deals that Guy was so often associated with.

Still, Chuck had a nagging question. "Why did Guy invite me here just to present an offer?" he thought. "Sure, it's nice to present an offer in person when it's convenient, but this hardly seems like the best use of our time. Maybe he's going to try to lowball me?"

As Chuck continued to process his thoughts, Guy pulled a file from his briefcase and smiled at Chuck, "You're probably wondering why I brought you all the way out here just to present an offer."

Just as before, Chuck nodded as Guy paused.

"Well, let's just say that my client asked me to conduct these negotiations with a certain level of discretion," Guy explained.

With that, Guy slid a stack of paperwork across the table to Chuck.

Chuck's eyes first went to the purchase amount. It was a full price offer. He then reviewed the remaining terms on the front page until he reached the buyer's name.

Chuck could not believe his eyes. He looked up at Guy to make sure this wasn't some kind of a joke. Surely, the name on the contract couldn't be that of the same woman who repeatedly appeared on nationally televised talk shows, had two best-selling books, and regularly functioned as an advisor to celebrities, politicians, and other high profile individuals.

This time it was Guy's turn to nod in affirmation.

"I try not to get involved in too many residential transactions," Guy explained. "But when an old friend called and made a special request I had a hard time saying no."

Now Chuck couldn't believe his ears. Not only was this prominent woman a client of Guy's, she was an old friend? An old friend that had specifically requested his help?

"Our businesses couldn't be more different," Chuck thought. This was the biggest transaction of Chuck's career and he had worked extremely hard to earn the listing. At the same time, this same transaction seemed almost inconsequential for Guy; a transaction that Guy was only a part of out of consideration for an old friend.

Chuck's eyes refocused on the offer in front of him and Guy continued, "My client is bringing 50% cash to the table and wants a quick close."

"This is literally too good to be true!" Chuck thought. While not consciously aware of it, he began to slowly shake his head.

"However, she does have one big request," Guy admitted. "She'd like to have the closing handled by a private attorney to ensure a reasonable degree of confidentiality. She's not trying to hide the purchase from anyone; she'd just like to avoid unnecessary media attention."

As crazy as this all seemed, Chuck felt like he was beginning to understand what was going on. He and Guy talked through the rest of the documents and Chuck agreed to present the offer to his seller as soon as he could.

Moments later their food arrived. As the server set everything in front of them Guy said, "Chuck, I hope you enjoy oysters as much as I do. But in case you don't, I had them bring out some of their famous smoked salmon."

"This week the chef had some fresh Kumamoto Oysters flown in from Willapa Bay in Washington State and they're to die for," Guy said excitedly. "As far as their salmon goes, I guarantee you've never had better."

"Actually, I like both," Chuck replied.

The ensuing minutes were filled with silence as the two men indulged their palettes.

Finally, Guy reengaged Chuck with a question, "So tell me Chuck, how's business?"

"Business is good," Chuck answered quickly, "very good, in fact. I'm on pace to have my best year yet."

"Excellent," exclaimed Guy. He then followed with another question. "How long have you been in the industry?"

"About five years," replied Chuck. "Prior to that, I was a sales rep for an out-of-state medical technology company. I did pretty well for myself in medical sales, but I decided that I wanted to have more control over my own destiny."

"So, do you?" Guy asked with a sparkle in his eyes.

"Do you now feel that you have more control over your destiny?"

Chuck was surprised by the direct question. Because of his recent end of the month experience and heart-to-heart conversation with Max, he still harbored strong feelings about this topic. As a result, a wave of nervous energy rushed over his body and he did his best to hide it as he responded.

"Sure," he answered, "I mean I feel like I do. I get to call all the shots and I like the fact that I'm accumulating wealth for myself instead of a group of unknown stockholders."

"Yes," said Guy slowly. His friendly gaze and subdued tone seemed to invite Chuck to elaborate further.

"Of course, we all have those moments when things feel a little out of control," Chuck continued.

After pausing for a moment, Chuck finally confessed, "I've actually had a few more of them than I'd like lately."

"But," he was quick to add, "I'm confident that I can work past them."

Chuck looked down at his plate for a brief moment and then back up again. "I guess the most frustrating thing for me is my time. I always hit my deadlines, but the cost in terms of my personal and professional time is significant and it impacts every area of my life."

"Interesting," said Guy, "very interesting."

"You impress me Chuck. Your professionalism and the amount energy you put into your business demand a lot of respect," Guy continued.

"Overall, the challenges that you are experiencing are the very same challenges that plague most top agents. In fact, I faced many of them as my business grew," Guy shared.

Guy's words of affirmation struck a chord with Chuck. His outward composure remained calm and professional, but inside he was grinning from ear to ear.

"Chuck, I've got a business proposition for you," Guy stated in matter-of-fact tone.

Chuck's ears immediately perked up. "There's more?" he thought to himself.

Guy continued, "Years ago, at the moment when I needed it the most, someone came along and shared some business principles with me that unlocked my true potential and completely transformed by real estate business."

"These principles came in the form of a Challenge. A Challenge that required a strong personal commitment and forced me to look at my business in a whole new way," Guy elaborated.

"Where can this be going?" wondered Chuck.

Guy seemed to read his mind and was ready with an answer.

"Chuck, I'd be honored to share these principles with you," Guy stated. "I am offering you a chance to take the Freedom Challenge."

Chuck didn't intend to hesitate, but he couldn't help it. There was no doubt that he wanted to learn how Guy had become so successful. At the same time, he wasn't sure what he was being asked to commit to.

Guy continued to demonstrate an uncanny ability to sense Chuck's unspoken questions, "The Freedom Challenge involves two coaching sessions with me and one-on-one meetings with three world class subject matter experts that will make the principles I share with you come to life."

"It concludes with a special assignment, but that's all I can tell you," Guy shared. The rest you'll have to experience for yourself. That is, if you accept."

Chuck was intrigued, but this all sounded too good to be true. He wasn't one for being taken advantage of or pushed into something.

"What's the catch," Chuck asked himself.

"No catch," answered Guy.

Although Chuck hadn't articulated his question verbally, Guy knew his thoughts. Guy knew them because they were identical to his own several decades earlier.

"I'm not looking for a coaching fee or a share of your future revenue," Guy explained. "But, there are two requirements."

"First, you must keep a journal and write down everything from our two coaching sessions and each of the one-on-one meetings you have."

"Second, at some point in your career, you must share the Freedom Challenge with at least one other person."

"Of course, there are no strings attached if you say no," Guy stated with his trademark smile.

From that point on there would be no more explanations to bail Chuck out. Guy leaned back comfortably in his chair, crossed his legs, and waited silently for Chuck's response.

Chuck knew what he wanted to say, but he took commitments very seriously and didn't want to rush into this one without careful consideration.

"I accept," Chuck finally proclaimed. "I'm not sure I

fully understand what I'm getting myself into, but if these are the same principles that are responsible for your success then I want to know what they are."

"Great," said Guy before Chuck could analyze his decision further. "I'd like to get started right away. Can you meet me back here on Monday at 4pm for our first coaching session?"

"Yes," answered Chuck as he used his phone to check his calendar.

"Monday it is then," Guy said. "I'll see you at 4 pm. Don't forget to bring your journal and be sure to dress comfortably. We won't spend much time indoors."

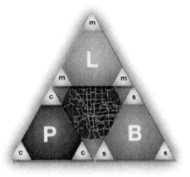

# CHAPTER **FOUR**

**W**arm sunshine greeted Chuck as he emerged from his vehicle. There were far fewer cars in the parking lot of the Beaumont Golf and Country Club than there had been on Friday. Just as Chuck was getting ready to pluck his golf clubs from his trunk he heard the distinctive sound of Guy's voice.

"Hey Chuck, over here," Guy called out.

Chuck looked to his left and saw Guy standing in front his luxury SUV motioning for Chuck to join him. By the time Chuck made his way over, Guy was ready for him with what appeared to be a shoe box.

"Here, try these on," Guy suggested.

Chuck opened the box to find a new pair of hiking shoes. He then looked up to Guy with a perplexed look on his face.

"You're starting a new journey today and I just wanted you to have a new pair of shoes," Guy said with a playful look on his face.

Chuck wasn't convinced.

"Seriously, I didn't want to give away my plans for our first coaching session by telling you what to bring so I took a guess at your shoe size when we met on Friday," Guy admitted. "If those don't fit I have a few other sizes."

The shoes fit Chuck's feet perfectly. Not only was the brand name unfamiliar to him, but he had never experienced anything like them. They felt like a lightweight running shoe, but had the appearance and strength of a durable, low rise hiking boot.

"These are really nice," Chuck said, almost to himself.

"Yes they are," said Guy. With that he reached into his SUV and tossed Chuck a new, brown and tan, nylon windbreaker that bore the same unfamiliar brand. "You may need this as well."

"A former client of mine is an equity partner in the company that has exclusive rights to market this particular line of sporting goods in the US," Guy explained. "He gave me a bunch of footwear and clothing samples from their upcoming product launch to distribute to my friends and family members. It's all top quality gear."

"I'll say," commented Chuck. "What's next?"

"Well, we'd better get going," Guy replied. "Why don't you drop your old shoes off at your car, grab your journal, and meet me at the entrance to the parking lot?"

When Chuck rejoined Guy, he noticed something that he'd failed to observe earlier. Across the street from the Beaumont Golf and Country Club was a small trail head. A small, unadorned sign next to it welcomed visitors and hikers to the Grader Creek Nature Preserve.

Guy gestured with a sweep of his hand, "Please, be my guest." With that the two men crossed the street and entered the preserve.

"Chuck, since we only have limited time together, I'm going be rather direct with you. Is that ok?" Guy asked.

Chuck nodded, "Sure, fine with me."

"Good," said Guy. "For the sake of our meeting today, I'm going to assume that you have a strong desire to be best you can be and operate your business in the most efficient and effective manner possible. I do respect what you've already accomplished, but I'm assuming you want more."

While it was nice to hear Guy say this, Chuck felt that he actually meant it. The fact that Guy communicated sincerely, without a hint of superiority or pretense, made it very easy for Chuck to cede control of the conversation.

"Your assumption is correct," Chuck affirmed. "I'm ready for whatever you've got."

Guy stopped walking. "Chuck, I can tell you from experience that what got you to where you are today, won't get you to where you want to go tomorrow."

"The ability of your business to grow is determined by the quality of the plan you use to guide your efforts. The problem is that most agents get started without a plan."

"Talented agents like you have so much drive and determination that they overcome this plan related deficiency with hard work. However, even when they see the need for a better plan, the one that they implement tends to be reactive instead of proactive."

"Despite a homegrown plan like this, a talented agent can reach a very respectable level of production. The downside is that the operating costs for such a plan are always much higher than they should be and growth becomes more and more painful with each transaction added. To accommodate change, these ad hoc plans require constant maintenance."

Before Guy could continue, both he and Chuck were forced to duck as two chirping swallows fighting over a twig swooped down from a nearby tree.

"Fortunately, there's a better way," Guy shared. "In fact, the plants and animals that surround us hold the key."

"Most agents have a single plan for lead generation or a single plan for growth but they're missing a plan that covers it all. You need a simple, holistic plan that has the ability to grow with your business without changing."

"Such a plan will not only accommodate the inevitable complexity that comes with business growth, but it will orchestrate it," Guy stated with emphasis.

Overall, Chuck felt like he understood the functionality that Guy was explaining, but he wasn't sure how all this was connected to Mother Nature.

"Inside every cell of every living organism is a plan, a special set of instructions called DNA," Guy continued.

"The first amazing thing about DNA is that it uses very simple building blocks and simple processes to coordinate very complex activities."

"The second remarkable feature of DNA is that the same set of instructions is used whether the organism has 1 cell or 1 trillion cells."

Guy waved his hand toward a tree, "Take this oak tree for example. Many decades ago, it began as an acorn with a single cell. As the tree grew, it became more and more complex. Different types of cells were required for the trunk, its roots, and its leaves."

"Today, there is a good chance that it has more than a million cells. Yet, the instructions that were in the single acorn are identical to the instructions that are now in each of its million plus cells."

Chuck looked at the old oak tree as Guy spoke. It was truly amazing to think that one simple set of instructions was all that the entire tree needed. As his business had become more complex he'd been constantly forced to rethink his plan. The tree's plan was different. It didn't react to change, it proactively directed it.

"I get it," said Chuck. "My business needs its own DNA and I need to create it."

"Discover," said Guy in a gentle, but impassioned tone. "The set of instructions that your business needs doesn't need to be created. The ideal plan for your business already exists. In fact, it's woven into the very fabric of the Freedom Challenge. Your first task is to discover it. Once you've done that, then you must operate your business in a manner that fully aligns with it."

As Guy paused, Chuck took a moment to take everything in. So far, all that Guy had shared really seemed to make sense. Finally, when he was ready to continue he gave Guy a nod and said, "Ok."

"Great," said Guy. "Let's take this idea to the next level."

"The foundation of the Freedom Challenge is the Freedom Formula. The Freedom Formula contains instructions for each important element of your business and these instructions are divided into three principles: the People Principle, the Brand Principle, and the Leverage Principle. Got it?"

Chuck ran everything through his head just to make sure. "The ideal plan for my business is the Freedom Formula which contains three principles: the People Principle, the Brand Principle, and the Leverage Principle," he thought to himself.

"Yes," confirmed Chuck.

By this time Guy and Chuck had walked at least a mile and were approaching a fork in the trail.

"How do the shoes feel," asked Guy looking down at Chuck's feet.

"Couldn't be more comfortable," Chuck responded, "which way?"

Guy motioned toward the path on the left which appeared to be less frequently traveled. "This one will take us where we want to go," he added.

"Now, let's move on to…" started Guy.

"Forgive me for interrupting Guy, but I want to circle back to the Freedom Formula," said Chuck in an apologetic, but direct tone.

"I understand that the People Principle, the Brand Principle, and the Leverage Principle exist and that they are important, but what are they? I don't feel like I have a good grasp of what they represent."

"Ah, I see," said Guy. "I don't want to get ahead of myself, but I suppose I could give you a brief description of each one. The three subject matter experts that you'll meet will cover each of these three areas in vivid detail."

With that, Guy looked off into the distance as if searching for his next thought. Finally, it appeared as though he found it.

"Business in general can be a very de-humanizing enterprise," Guy began. "The words that we use to describe those that have the potential to patronize our services tend to reinforce this unfortunate tendency."

"The terms 'client' or 'customer' seem innocuous enough, but they still homogenize the otherwise unique traits that each individual possess. The words 'prospect' and 'lead' are even worse, they reduce individuals to mere objects."

"To combat this, the individuals that patronize your services, or have the potential to patronize your services, must be recognized, first and foremost, for what they are: human beings.

"The People Principle instructs you to orient your business around people as human beings and lays out three powerful methods of interacting with them. Quite literally, the People Principle will open your eyes to a whole host of new, very profitable opportunities."

Chuck seemed to be tracking, so Guy continued, "The Brand Principle, as you may have guessed, is related to the marketing."

"Most agents perform poorly in this area because they assume that a brand is nothing more than a name or logo. Nothing could be further from the truth. As the Brand Principle outlines, your brand is the core of your overall marketing strategy and is manifested in every aspect of your business."

Again, Guy's gaze drifted toward the skyline. When he resumed he spoke hesitantly.

"It's difficult to do the Leverage Principle justice in just a few minutes. It's a powerful, yet simple concept that can easily be disregarded or overlooked."

"In many ways, employing leverage in your business gives you super human ability. You won't gain the ability to fly or make yourself invisible, but the Leverage Principle, and the three concepts associated with it will drive your personal production through the roof."

"I hope this helps, but feel like I've said too much already. I don't want to get ahead of myself. Again, you'll learn a lot more about these concepts in the coming weeks," said Guy.

Just then, they rounded a corner and below them a large, beautiful valley unfolded. In the heart of the valley, they could clearly see a few homes, a farmhouse or two, and an old country school.

Chuck had been aware that they had been gaining elevation as they walked, but he never would have guessed that they had climbed high enough to enjoy this kind of a view.

About ten feet behind Chuck and Guy stood two

benches. Local volunteers had constructed them out of fallen trees following a major windstorm the following winter. The benches were situated so that hikers could pause and take in the splendor below.

"Do you mind if we stop so I can write some of this down?" Chuck asked pulling out his journal.

"Be my guest," replied Guy. He then waited for Chuck to jot down all that he had learned about the Freedom Formula and its three principles: People, Brand, and Leverage.

As soon as Chuck was done, he looked up at Guy, ready for him to continue his lecture.

However, Guy had different plans. His eyes were focused on kids running and playing in the country schoolyard hundreds of feet below them.

"Chuck, when was the last time you played?" Guy asked.

"I'm sorry?" replied Chuck. He wasn't sure what Guy was getting at.

Guy pressed further, "When was the last time you let go, had some fun, and played hard? I'm talking about running, playing hide-and-go-seek with your kids, a board game, whatever. When was the last time you played Chuck?"

Chuck scratched his head. He'd played a lot of games with his children when they were younger, but he hadn't done anything like that in years. When he and Glori had first been married they had enjoyed a lot of active recreation together, but that too had subsided.

Now that he thought about it, Chuck couldn't remember the last time he'd played. It certainly hadn't been in the five years that had passed since he had become a real estate agent.

Chuck's silence served as his confession.

"Chuck, you're not alone," Guy shared. "Few adults engage in genuine play. The problem with this is that most people's sense of creativity and wonder is lost along with it."

"Without play, adults begin to look at life one dimensionally. We see problems instead of opportunities. We focus on our shortcomings instead of our strengths. We voluntarily build prisons for our minds with serious sounding words like obligation and duty.

"Pretty soon this narrow thinking leads to an inability to separate fact from opinion. When we are unable to separate fact from opinion we draw conclusions about our world that aren't necessarily true. These erroneous conclusions have only one outcome, to hold us back both personally and professionally."

"Ultimately, we get stuck doing things the way we've always done them. We assume that the rules of the game are set and that we must operate within them."

"Let me give you an example. A new agent is working with a very particular set of buyers. These buyers have him running all over town, going this way and that. When they find a new house, they want the agent to show it to them immediately. When they call, the agent drops whatever he is doing to help them."

"Now, if you asked him, he'd say he doesn't have a choice," Guy stated. "He'd tell you that these are just the rules of real estate and that the customer is always right."

"Of course, top agents aren't going to have this same problem, but they can wind up getting just as stuck in other parts of their business," Guy added.

"Here is a different example. When a child falls down on the playground he doesn't consider himself a failure, he just picks himself up and jumps back in the fray."

"As adults, when we stumble or fall, we're tempted to think that we are somehow inherently flawed. Unfortunately, when we associate our mistakes with our identity we literally sentence ourselves to repeat the unwanted behavior."

Chuck wasn't ready to openly admit falling prey to either of these scenarios, but he could see the point that Guy was making.

"So, what's the answer?" Chuck asked. "Do I need to go run around a playground once a week?

Guy smiled, "Yes and no. There's more than one kind of playground and you'll need to play more than once a week. Daily is more like it."

"You see Chuck, when we play we suspend what we believe to be reality. This allows us to see our world without limits. Then, the creative process of constructing a new world with new rules becomes the act of play itself."

As Guy spoke Chuck eye's drifted to the playground below. He watched as a group of children ran around with their arms out pretending that they were airplanes.

Without thinking he suddenly interrupted Guy, "You're right, that is exactly the way that children think and act when they are at play."

"Precisely," Guy agreed.

"The bottom line is this Chuck, without an active and curious mind that is fed by regular play, we have no chance of seeing all the possibilities that exist for our businesses. What's worse, we end up trapped in a lifetime of self-imposed drudgery."

"For this reason, the Freedom Challenge is constructed like a game. You'll learn how to play the game by meeting with me and by engaging one-on-one with the each of the three subject matter experts. After that you'll begin playing the game with the instructions I've provided."

Guy could tell that he was losing Chuck, but he knew this was inevitable the first time around. He decided to make concept of playing more personal.

"The type of play that is required to set you free is found in your dreams and aspirations. I'm not taking about your business goals. I'm referring to your really big, lifelong dreams."

"Of course, if you haven't thought about them in a while you may not remember what they are or, if you do remember them, chances are you don't see them as realistic or possible."

Chuck nodded to confirm that, for the most part, this was true.

"Chuck, I'm going to ask you three questions, but I don't want you to answer them right now. I simply want you to write them in your journal. Here they are..."

Chuck flipped a page in his journal and was ready to

write.

"Number one. What would you do with your life if you had more than enough money and didn't need to work?" said Guy.

Pausing briefly, Guy continued with the next question, "Number two. What would you do if you knew you couldn't fail? I mean anything Chuck."

When Chuck looked up, Guy began again, "Number three. What makes you come alive?"

"All three of these questions are closely connected to the real purpose behind the Freedom Challenge," Guy continued.

"They point toward what I call the Higher Purpose of Business…" Guy trailed off. "Actually, I'm getting ahead of myself again. Let's stop here. This will all make a lot more sense and will have greater impact when we have our final coaching session."

Chuck was confused and more than a bit curious. This was more information than he had anticipated and the lack of closure bothered him.

Guy seemed to sense this. "Chuck, I don't normally talk a lot about the idea of play and the Higher Purpose of Business when I meet with someone for the first time." he confessed. "So, it would make sense if you are still wondering how all of this fits."

"Right now working and playing must seem like they belong at opposite ends of the spectrum. For most people they are. The problem is that most people aren't free. The closer you get to completing the Freedom Challenge, the more you'll see that combining these two isn't really something you do, it's a by-product of running your business and your life according to the Freedom Formula."

Based on Guy's explanation, Chuck knew that he'd have to take some of this on faith. Still, he reserved the right to remain skeptical.

Guy looked down at his watch. "We'd better get going," he remarked. "To finish the loop, and get back to the trailhead, we've got to cover a little more than two miles."

As they made their way back, Guy gave Chuck plenty of time to think about the concepts that they had discussed. He knew the danger of trying to feed someone too much information early on in the Challenge.

# 1st Meeting with Guy

Lessons Learned:

1. My business needs a Plan.

   But, it needs to be a

   ## HOLISTIC PLAN

2. Freedom Formula = The Plan

   It already exists...I don't need to create it!

3 Parts

Leverage

People ——— Brand

3. Play is not only fun but it is essential and it can help me be more productive.

These questions will help me discover my Higher Purpose of Business.

A. What would I do if I had enough money and didn't have to work?

B. What would I do if I knew I couldn't fail?

C. What makes me come alive?

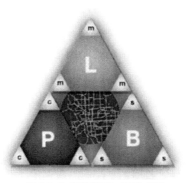

## CHAPTER **FIVE**

It was nearly impossible for Guy to walk through the parking lot of the Beaumont Golf and Country Club and not see someone he knew. As a consequence, Chuck and Guy stopped several times to deliver a quick handshake and a 'hello' on the way back to their vehicles.

When they finally reached Guy's SUV, Chuck turned to thank him.

"Guy, I appreciate the time you spent with me today," Chuck said. "I'm not sure I fully understand how everything fits, but I am willing to stick with it for the time being. The assumption I'm making is that you are teaching me the same principles that led to your success."

"They are," affirmed Guy. "Chuck, before you go there's something else I'd like to share with you.  Do you have a moment?"

"Sure," Chuck responded.

With that, Guy motioned for Chuck to follow him to the back of his vehicle. He opened the back gate to retrieve a small object which he then handed to Chuck.

"Chuck, what did I just give you?" Guy asked.

"A magnifying glass?" Chuck answered with a puzzled expression.

"Had that one since I was a kid," Guy added. "My grandfather gave it to me for my eighth birthday and then he spent a whole afternoon showing me how to use it. One of my favorite things to do was to position it over a leaf or piece of paper and burn a hole using only sun light. Did you ever do anything like that?"

Chuck smiled, "Yes, I believe I did. It's been a long time though."

"This may be a simple illustration, but it's one of the best ways to demonstrate the power of focus," Guy shared.

"The sun's rays have to travel more than 92 million miles to reach us. When they leave the sun their temperature is 27 million degrees Fahrenheit, but by the time they hit the earth the rays are so spread out that they only have a moderate warming effect. They've lost their focus and their potency."

"A magnifying glass is just a simple tool that helps the sun recover a little of its focus by concentrating its rays on a specific target," Guy added.

After pausing for emphasis Guy continued, "There is a similar tool that is part of the Freedom Formula called a Primary Hub. In some ways it's a lot like a geographic farm. More importantly, it helps you focus the People Principle, the Brand Principle, and the Leverage Principle so that they have maximum effectiveness."

Chuck thought about this for a second and handed the magnifying glass back to Guy. "I've heard of other people doing farming, but I never wanted to limit myself. I want to reach as many people as possible and want to have the number one real estate business in town, not just in a neighborhood or two."

"Good point Chuck, good point," Guy responded. "So the question is, if you focus your efforts geographically, are you limiting yourself?"

Chuck nodded to gesture that was indeed the question.

"Chuck, tell me, do you know how many people live in our little town?" Guy asked.

"221,000 people not including those that have moved

here since the last census," Chuck answered. He was able to reply quickly because he had just been looking at these figures last week with his title rep.

"Impressive," said Guy. He had respect for those that knew their numbers. "I want to share something with you that may not sound shocking at first, but it will be when we compare it to the population figure you provided."

"The average American is exposed to $376.62 of advertising each year and this figure continues to rise annually. Let's say you were to spend $221,000 on advertising that was targeted at our entire town over the next year. If you did so, you'd reach each person with $1 of advertising. Does that sound right?"

Chuck quickly did the math in his head, "221,000 people divided by $221,000 equals $1 per person. Yes, that is correct."

Guy was ready with his punch line, "So, here's where the rubber fails to hit the road. Your $1 per person of advertising represents less than 0.3% of the total advertising that citizens in our town are exposed to. They are not going to hear your messages, because the remaining $375.62 of advertising will drown you out."

The writing on the wall was growing clearer and

Chuck nodded for Guy to continue.

"Chuck, based on this, I've got to ask you two questions. Are you prepared to spend $211,000 on advertising next year and, even if you are, would you be happy with the level of effectiveness I just described?"

"No, I don't even plan to spend a tenth of that and, when you frame it that way, the answer to the second question is clearly no," Chuck responded.

"Good," said Guy. "Now, let's narrow the focus of your advertising and see what we get."

"Every time you cut your target population in half, you double the marketing messages that each person is exposed to even while spending the same amount of money. If you focus on 50% of the population then you can send the equivalent of two messages per person, if you focus on 25% then you can send the equivalent of four messages person, and so on."

Chuck was getting a little impatient, "So, what's the answer?"

"Greater focus," answered Guy. "You want to drive up the messages per person until your messages can be heard well above the noise of the market. The rule of thumb that I teach is to keep cutting your population in half and keeping doubling your messages until you get to

1000 homes. In our town, this represents roughly 1-2% of the population."

Chuck understood the overall concept, but still felt like he was missing something. "So, I just go out and pick any 1000 homes?" he asked.

"No, I'm glad you asked. There are a lot of factors that you'll want to consider like character of the neighborhood, the median sale price, and the sales turnover percentage. I actually have a list of criteria to give you, but I'll save that for our last meeting."

Guy continued, "We still need to answer your earlier question Chuck. We've clearly demonstrated that marketing and advertising becomes much more effective when it is focused. But, does this geographic focus limit your business growth?"

Before Chuck could respond Guy provided an answer. "The answer is no. Once you've built up market share in a given area, you are able to select a new area to focus on. The key is to completely saturate an area before you branch out into a new one."

Chuck considered this idea for a moment. "Sounds like the game of Risk," he said thoughtfully.

"It's a lot like Risk, but that's another topic for our final meeting" said Guy. "However, it's safe to say that if you spread yourself too thin you'll never establish permanent market share. You've got to build a stronghold of a 1000 homes before you move on to conquer new territory."

Guy paused for emphasis, "These 1000 homes will represent your Primary Hub. This is where the Freedom Challenge really begins. It all starts with focus.

As the two men parted, Chuck thanked Guy again for his time and Guy reminded Chuck to update his journal with their most recent conversation. He also handed Chuck a small piece of paper that contained information for Chuck's meeting with the first subject matter expert.

# Parking Lot with Guy

## Lessons Learned:

1. Focus = Primary Hub
   (Like Farming)

   It makes People, Brand,
   Leverage more effective

                Leverage

          (Hub)

   People ———— Brand

2. I want my message heard above
   the noise of the market.

   → 1000 homes = My Hub

3. I need to saturate my Hub
   before I branch out.

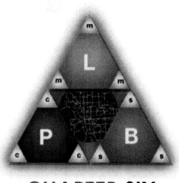

# CHAPTER SIX

Traffic was bumper to bumper as Chuck made his way to a small college on the west side of town. He glanced at his watch and knew he was going to be late. Just when his patience had hit its limit, traffic broke free and he reached his exit.

Soon he spotted the classic looking brick buildings that housed Benson College. Just over the tops of the trees he could see the lights that towered above his destination, Veteran's Memorial Field.

As Chuck parked he could see the football team already beginning their pre-practice warm-ups. "It's odd that my appointment is at 3pm, isn't this the middle of practice," he thought.

Then Chuck recalled his earlier conversation with

Guy. "You'll never meet anyone like the Coach, his methods aren't exactly conventional," Guy had said.

Chuck had then asked, "I've always wondered does the Coach have a real name?"

Guy had smiled and replied, "Sure he does, but no one ever uses it except the Coach himself. His last name is Raymond and he's a legend."

And a legend he was. Chuck had been reading about the Coach in the sports section of the local newspaper for more than 30 years. As far as he could remember the Coach had never had a losing season.

The Coach's teams were always exciting to watch and each year it seemed as though they were consistently competing for some kind of league or divisional championship. On top of all this, the Coach had even won a handful of national small college football titles during his storied career.

The shrill sound of a whistle blowing brought Chuck back to reality and he quickly looked down at his watch. It was 2:57 pm and that meant he was seven minutes late by his standards. He knew he had better get going.

Grabbing his bag he jumped from the car and walked briskly toward the classic looking gymnasium across the street. Just as he reached the main entrance, a kind-looking, middle-aged gentleman exited from one of the doors. He smiled as he held the door open for Chuck.

As Chuck passed through the door he turned and asked, "Say, is the Coach's office close by?

"Sure is" replied the man, "but if it's after 3 pm and you'll find him out on the football field. My name's Eddie and I'm headed that way myself. I'd be happy to walk you out there."

Chuck felt relieved and uncomfortable at the same time. He was grateful for the escort, but he was beginning to think that the Freedom Challenge wasn't for him.

What was he thinking? He didn't want to be out in the middle of a football practice. He was here to learn how to master his real estate business and take control of his life; he wasn't sure what a football coach had to do with any of this. This whole thing was beginning to seem like a big mistake.

As quickly as they started, his rapid fire thoughts were interrupted by a question.

"What brings you to meet with Coach Raymond?" Eddie asked.

"Honestly, I'm not sure," Chuck confessed. "My name is Chuck Stevens and a gentleman by the name of Guy

Chamberlain invited me to participate in an odd sort of Challenge. One of first things I'm supposed to do is meet with the Coach to learn about a very important business concept."

Chuck continued, "Do you know Coach Raymond well?"

Eddie chuckled, "I've know him for many years, what can I tell you about him?"

Chuck could hardly believe his ears and decided to take advantage of an opportunity to obtain some valuable background information so that he could impress the Coach during their meeting.

"Well, I guess I'm wondering what makes the Coach so successful," Chuck asked.

"Now, that is an interesting question," Eddie replied. "Do you have some time to sit on the bleachers and talk for few minutes?"

By now the two men had walked to the edge of the field where practice was officially beginning. A few of the assistant coaches had broken the team into two groups at opposite ends of the field, but Chuck didn't see any sign of the Coach. Since it was clear that the Coach hadn't arrived yet, he readily accepted Eddie's offer.

As they found their seats, Chuck looked up and

caught a glimpse of the snowcapped peaks of the nearby mountain range.

"What a great view," Chuck commented.

Eddie nodded and smiled in agreement before he gently redirected the conversation with a single word.

"People," said Eddie.

Chuck repeated the same word hesitantly, "People?"

"That's right," Eddie answered.

"What's right?" Chuck asked.

"The secret to Coach Raymond's success is people," Eddie replied, "It is all about people."

"Do you mean his players?" Chuck pressed, "His success must be due to more than just the quality of his players."

"Oh, it's due to much more than the quality of his players, although they're some of the best small college football players in the country," Eddie stated.

After pausing for a moment Eddie continued, "Let me tell you a story about Coach Raymond. One that he is not too proud of."

"When he was seventeen years old Coach Raymond was a star quarterback and the captain of his high school football team. College scouts came from around the country to watch him play."

"On the outside he was everything you would expect from the captain of a varsity football team and he knew it too. In his own words, 'His oversized ego outweighed the lineman that blocked for him'," Eddie shared.

"As a result he treated people like objects; if they weren't useful to him they were quickly disposed of," Eddie stated.

"Then one Friday night his life changed forever. He was playing the game of his life in front of a sold out crowd and had just thrown his fifth touchdown pass when an opposing player tripped and crashed into his right leg. The doctor said it was the worst compound fracture he had ever seen and that Coach Raymond would be lucky to walk again."

"The worst part wasn't the pain or the career ending injury. It was the fact that not one of his teammates came to visit him." Eddie paused for emphasis, "not one."

"In fact, when he was finally able to join his team on the sidelines at the end of the season they had all but forgotten about him."

"Over the next year Coach Raymond would learn the greatest lesson that life could teach him," Eddie paused again.

"If you treat people like they are disposable then you

become disposable yourself."

"Shortly afterward, he rededicated his life to the game of football…but this time as a coach and with a radically different outlook. The rest, as we say, is history."

Lost in the story, Chuck had almost forgotten why he was he was there. Before he could think of something to say Eddie continued.

"This may seem surprising to you but Coach Raymond's number one goal isn't winning," Eddie stated. "His top goal is to honor his fellow coaches, his players, the training staff, the janitorial staff, bus drivers, and just about anyone else he comes in contact with.

"The funny thing is, the more he honors other people, the more he seems to win," Eddie commented. "He is so serious about honoring the people around him that he actually has a formula for it. The formula itself is simple, but it requires intentional effort to execute it."

"The formula is: Contribution, Communication, and Connection. We call them the three 'C's of the People Principle."

Chuck suddenly remembered that Guy had reminded him to bring his journal so that he could take notes. Hurriedly, he retrieved it from his bag and began writing as Eddie spoke.

"Contribution is the first 'C' and it reminds us that one of the primary ways to honor others is through giving."

"You see we live in world full of entitlement in which most people feel like they're owed something. When we think and act like this we push away the people that have the potential to help us the most."

"Coach Raymond's success is directly associated with the level of his Contribution, how much he gives. In fact, he's been known to remind others from time to time that, 'Giving begins the receiving process.' But, don't be confused, he doesn't give just to receive and neither should you."

"If you think that way then you limit yourself to the game of addition and subtraction. All you are doing is trading one favor for another. You'll never get ahead that way."

"You need multiplication on your side and that is exactly what happens when your Contributions to others come from your heart without any strings attached. The return you end up getting is multiplied many times over and it happens in ways that you could never predict. Sincere giving is a magical thing!"

Chuck was nodding and writing as fast as he could.

Eddie was now in his groove and words flowed from his lips with ease.

"The next 'C' is Communication. Communication is the lifeblood of relationships and relationships are as critical in the world of business as they are in the world of sports. Any company or team will wither and die without the cooperation that ensues from healthy relationships."

"Many impatient people think that they can just manipulate and use people to get what they want without investing in relationships. This kind of short sided thinking may produce some good looking short term results, but these strategies all backfire eventually."

"If you want to build a successful business or team, there is no substitute for building relationships. And, if you want to build relationships there is no substitute for Communication."

"Think of it this way Chuck, if relationships were sold in the grocery store they'd come in a box, they'd be dehydrated, and the directions on the back would say, 'Just Add Communication'."

"The funny thing about Communication is that we can't just communicate when we want or need something. Imagine if I never spoke to my wife except to make demands or requests, what kind of a relationship would she and I have?"

"The importance of Communication can be summed up in two words: Frequency and Impact."

"Coach Raymond communicates with his players and their parents more than 33 times throughout the year. Whether it's the newsletter his staff sends out, a personal email, or a quick phone call, he's always looking to positively impact the lives of his players, their families, and the community at large."

"Yes sir, the second 'C' is Communication and it's a big one," Eddie said with emphasis.

Chuck was so hooked that he immediately blurted out, "What about the last 'C'?"

Eddie grinned, "I thought you'd never ask? Connection. Connection is the last 'C' and boy is it important. People need to know and trust that you have their best interest in mind. If you can't establish this level of rapport then you'll never win big."

"You've got to get into the trenches and coexist with the people you want to work with. You've got to Connect with them on their level and on their terms."

"Such a perspective allows you to truly understand

the unique challenges and needs that others face. And, it is precisely this viewpoint that allows you to identify hidden opportunities that can't be seen any other way."

"When people see that you don't have an ulterior motive, and they truly feel understood, then you are able to Connect with them in a personal, authentic, and productive way. It is this form of Connection that literally allows you to create and capitalize on new opportunities."

With that Eddie gave his new friend a few moments to digest his message.

As Chuck looked up from his journal he realized that he hadn't even gotten a chance to meet the Coach yet. Even worse, he didn't even have an idea of what time it was. He glanced at his watch and saw that it was nearly 4 pm.

Just as Chuck was getting ready to speak, a whistle blew and a tall man with a hat called over to the bleachers.

"Hey Coach, the offense and defense have completed their workouts. I think their ready for you and then we'll finish up with a special teams run through," the tall man yelled.

Eddie stood and replied, "Sounds great Tom, get

everyone together on the fifty yard line and I'll be down in a moment."

Slowly, a sense of realization swept over Chuck, "Wait a minute, you're the Coach?"

"You got me," Eddie confessed. "Eddie is my name, Eddie Raymond. And right now I've got an entire football team waiting for me."

"Chuck, I hope you found what you came for and I must say it has been a sincere pleasure speaking with you," Eddie said.

With that, Eddie turned to go. However, when he reached the bottom of the bleachers he stopped to offer some parting advice.

"Remember, if you treat people like they are disposable then you become disposable yourself. When you stick with the 3 'C's: Contribution, Communication, and Connection, then you can't go wrong."

Chuck was awestruck. As he drove home he shook his head at the unbelievable turn of events. He couldn't wait to share everything with Glori, but he wasn't sure he could fully describe the magic of the afternoon. Plus, she had been rather skeptical when he had told her about his hike with Guy the week prior.

That night before he went to bed Chuck pulled out

his journal and reviewed his notes one last time.

# Meeting with the Coach

Lessons Learned:

1. People = Success

   If I treat people like they are disposable, I become disposable myself.

2. There is a special formula for honoring people called the three C's of the People Principle.

Leverage

People — Brand

Hub

3. 1st C = Contribution

Giving starts the receiving process, but don't expect something in return

Think <u>Multiplication!</u>

4. 2nd C = Communication

Communication is the lifeblood of Relationships with People

Think Frequency & Impact!

5. 3rd C = Connection

Get in the trenches with People. Seek to understand.

It will help me see opportunities that are otherwise unseen.

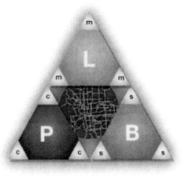

# CHAPTER **SEVEN**

"This is Chuck," Chuck stated mechanically as he answered his phone for what seemed to be the one hundredth time that afternoon. The conversation ended up being one of the many routine phone exchanges that Chuck engaged in during the average work week.

The last several days had brought with them a whirlwind of activity. In fact, he had been so busy that he had nearly forgotten about his meeting the prior week with the Coach and for that matter, the Freedom Challenge itself.

There was a long to-do list of messages to respond to, active buyers to appease, seller prospects to call, listings to preview, and a very long list of other amorphous items. For all intents and purposes this to-do list was never-ending. This to-do list was his life.

Then it happened. Chuck was instantly drawn back into the Freedom Challenge by a small piece of paper.

As he retrieved Friday's mail from his inbox, he sifted through it in his usual fashion. This meant that he positioned himself over his recycle bin and effortlessly let the advertisements and solicitations fall from his hands never again to be seen by human eyes.

Bills and invoices went into one pile, title policies and mortgage paperwork into another and miscellaneous items into a third.

Authentic personal correspondence was somewhat rare and depending on his mood he would either toss it in the miscellaneous pile or take a moment to quickly inspect its contents.

At first glance there was nothing unusual about the stack of mail he held; a bill from the sign company, yet another title policy, and then there it was.

In between a letter from his local MLS and what looked to be another bill was a small, embossed envelope with a unique seal.

As he turned the envelope over he was impressed by both the weight and refined texture of the paper. After gently lifting the seal he withdrew a single piece of cardstock.

It was an invitation. The card read:

*To: Mr. and Mrs. Charles Stevens*
*From: The Salebra House*
*Re: A Day In The Clouds*

*Unsurpassed natural beauty awaits as you heed the call of renewal and transformation. Mr. Terry Jacobs has personally requested your presence for a day of rejuvenation followed by a private dining experience.*

*Preparations are being made for your arrival on the evening of Friday October 5th. Enclosed is a card with my personal phone extension should you need to reach me for any reason prior to your stay with us at the House in the Clouds.*

*With delight,*

*Grace De Lamarliere*
*Director of Guest Experiences*
*The Salebra House*

This was unlike any correspondence he had ever received from a business. Everything about the invitation, down to the last detail, was perfect. The handwritten message itself had been painstakingly penned by a talented calligraphist.

As fate would have it, Chuck was so busy that he didn't have another chance to think about the invitation until he was positioned behind the wheel of his foreign luxury car and destined for the Salebra House.

He and Glori engaged in light-hearted conversation as the two-lane, mountain highway whisked them upwards like a giant escalator.

The world around them basked in the soft glow of the evening sun as the couple got caught up on everything from the outcome of Glori's recent meeting with their son's teacher to the scheduling of Chuck's upcoming annual eye exam.

All conversation stopped when they rounded a sharp, 180-degree turn in the road and came face to face with a handsome mountain lodge. It was flanked on both sides by a breathtaking view of the sun setting in the valley thousands of feet below them.

The wood and stone structure reminded Chuck of a hybrid between a rugged European castle and a chalet in the Swiss Alps.

Light radiated from every side of the building and beckoned them closer like a siren's song. Hardly aware of his actions, Chuck pulled his car around the circular drive and passed his keys to the valet as his car door was opened for him.

"Welcome to the Salebra House, Mr. Stevens, I'll take care of your car and your bags," the valet said with a warm smile. "Horace is inside waiting for you."

As if still under some hypnotic spell, Chuck didn't stop to ask how the man knew his name. Instead he turned to follow Glori as she made her way toward an enormous set of double doors.

"Mr. and Mrs. Steven's, my name is Horace, please allow me to show you to your table," said a kind, older gentlemen as he gestured gracefully with his arm.

Instead of walking into what they expected to be a standard hotel lobby, Chuck and Glori found themselves in a posh dining area at one end of a great hall.

There were no lines to wait in and no paperwork to complete. In the tables that surrounded them a spirited, but refined cocktail party appeared to be underway.

Horace stopped in front a small table for two, pulled out a chair, and invited Glori to sit. "Stanley, our wine steward will be with you in a moment," he said. "I've taken the liberty of ordering one of our chef's special appetizers for you and I'll be bringing it out in a moment."

Glori silently mouthed a single word to Chuck as

Horace turned to leave, "Unbelievable."

From the exceptional service offered by the Salebra House staff, to the harmony of the live violin and cello duo, to the exquisitely prepared cuisine, Chuck was in awe.

Neither he nor Glori had ever experienced anything like this. For an hour or two, time seemed to stand still.

Then, before he knew it, he was lying amid a luxurious collection of linens that covered their bed and was dreaming deeply.

Following an equally elegant and impressive breakfast for two, Glori donned a thick white robe before she headed off to the spa for a day of facial treatments, aromatherapy, and deep body massage.

In turn, Chuck was escorted to the study were he was greeted by a tall, stylish man in his middle 40's.

"Chuck, Terry Jacobs, it's great to meet you!" the man said. "Please sit down."

"Tell me about your stay," Terry asked as they reclined in two oversized chairs that were positioned on either side of a large crackling fire.

"I don't know where to begin," Chuck admitted. "I'm speechless. This place is simply amazing."

Terry grinned from ear-to-ear. "I can't tell you how happy I am to hear that. What you are experiencing is no accident. I've poured my life into making the guest experience here at the Salebra House one of a kind."

Before Chuck could interject Terry continued, "But you're not just here to experience what the Salebra House has to offer, you're here for the Freedom Challenge."

Chuck nodded as he sipped a mug of hot coffee that had been waiting for him. That was all the invitation Terry needed.

"Nearly ten years ago I left a mid six figure job as a Brand Manager for one of the biggest advertising firms in New York City. My firm was one of the top firms in its industry and I handled its most elite corporate clients. Companies didn't just come to me when they needed to put together a new promotion or marketing campaign, they came to me because I had a reputation for building incredibly strong brands."

"Why would you ever leave a job like that?" asked Chuck.

"Good question," replied Terry. "It's difficult to explain, but I finally decided I'd had enough of the rat race. As glamorous as business in the Big Apple may seem, the fast paced lifestyle doesn't come without a significant cost. I had always dreamed of owning and operating an establishment like this, but I couldn't quite bring myself to pull the trigger."

"The last string came during a winter trip to Switzerland. My wife and I had an incredible experience at a quaint chalet in the Alps. It was then and there that I decided I was going to make a change and put my branding experience directly to work for me. Shortly after that trip, I cashed in all my corporate stock and began to construct the Salebra House."

Given the similar rationale he had for his own career change Chuck seemed to comprehend this explanation. "How did you come up with the name Salebra House?" he queried.

Terry smiled, "I was wondering when you'd ask, but if I answer that question now I'll get ahead of myself. Let me ask you a question instead, what's the most important thing about a strong Brand?"

Chuck shrugged his shoulders indifferently.

Terry continued, "Differentiation. In fact, differentiation is the whole reason for branding."

For the moment this seemed reasonable, so Chuck wrote the word 'Differentiation' at the top of a new page in his journal.

"Chuck, you're in real estate aren't you?" Terry asked.

"Yes, for the last five years," Chuck answered.

Terry nodded and continued "Chuck, for a moment I want you to imagine a world in which every real estate agent is absolutely identical, a world in which you cannot distinguish one agent from another."

Chuck thought about it for a moment and finally said, "Ok."

"Good," Terry said. "Now image you are one of these nameless, faceless agents. If you want to attract more customers, what options do you have?"

"In the scenario you're describing I can't think any options aside from lowering my commission," Chuck said.

"Lowering your price is one option you have for increasing the number of customers you serve," Terry stated. "Now what happens if you lower your price?"

"I'll make less money, no money at all, or possibly lose money depending on the circumstances," Chuck replied.

"Right again," Terry said. "The only other option for attracting more customers is to work harder. But, when you take customers away from other agents, the other agents respond by lowering their prices. And, when other agents lower their prices your customers will demand lower prices or go elsewhere. Remember, you are nameless and faceless so your customers feel no loyalty to you."

Chuck gave Terry a nod to indicate that he understood so Terry continued.

"Chuck, in the same scenario, what will happen if you raise your commission above that of the other agents?" Terry asked.

"I'll lose customers," Chuck said. "Since we all look the same they'll just go with another agent who charges less."

"Yes," Terry replied. "Chuck, the hypothetical world we just described in which every real estate agent is completely identical, is called a Perfectly Competitive Marketplace."

"In a Perfectly Competitive Marketplace customers select the business they will patronize solely on price. A Perfectly Competitive Marketplace is a horrible environment for real estate agents or any business because they cannot change their net profit by changing their price."

"A business in a Perfectly Competitive Marketplace

can serve more customers if they lower their price, but they make less per customer so their profits stay the same. Similarly, if a business in a Perfectly Competitive Marketplace raises its prices it will make more per customer, but profits stay the same because they are serving fewer customers."

As Terry was getting ready to begin his next sentence Chuck waved his hand to interrupt him. The skeptic inside Chuck wasn't buying all that Terry was saying.

"Terry," Chuck started. "This doesn't all fit for me. I can think of plenty of business examples in which a company operates in a very competitive industry and they are able to increase their profits by changing their prices."

"Right you are Chuck," Terry agreed. "A Perfectly Competitive Marketplace is imaginary and will never exist in the real world."

"But," Terry continued. "The point you made brings up an interesting question. How do you think the companies in the business examples you are thinking of are able to increase their profits by changing their prices?"

Chuck hadn't given it much thought so he gave Terry a shrug.

"Branding," Terry said as he answered his own question. "They used Branding to make themselves different. Only after they differentiated themselves were they able to increase their profits by changing their prices."

By now Chuck's pen was moving furiously across the pages of his journal.

"Based on this, the goal for every company should be to differentiate itself from its competition to such a degree that it has no competition at all. When you don't have any immediate competition you get to set your own price and reap the profits."

All of this was ringing through to Chuck. He had watched many nameless real estate agents come and go. Nothing made them special and when their clients threatened to leave in search of lower fees they often reduced their commission significantly. They were powerless.

In his own right, he'd done all he could to distance himself from them, but he was open to learning how he could do more.

"I think a lot of real estate agents operate like they are in a Perfectly Competitive Marketplace." Chuck commented. "I've worked hard to distinguish myself from them, but it requires a lot of time and energy."

Terry seemed to understand. "I think you'll enjoy this quick lesson on Branding," he stated confidently.

"One of the first things I learned when I was getting my marketing degree was that your Brand is just a natural extension of your product. If your product looks like everyone else's product, then your Brand will look the same as well."

Chuck interjected, "and if my Brand is the same then I'm not far from being in a Perfectly Competitive Marketplace, I get that."

"Good" Terry affirmed. "Then let's talk about what it takes to make your Brand unique and different."

"There are three main elements. I call them the three 'S's of the Branding Principle: Skills, Standards, and Style."

"While the foundation of the Branding Principle is Skills, for the sake of our conversation today I think it makes sense to start off talking about Standards.

"During your stay here at the Salebra House one of the first things you witnessed was one of our Standards in action which is to greet our guests by name the moment they step out of their car."

Chuck thought back to his twilight arrival the night

before. "How are you able to do that?' he asked. "Before I ever identified myself the valet attendant already knew my name. It's almost like he recognized my car."

"He did," replied Terry. "You see, when the reservation is made we always get the make and model of the guest's vehicle along with the license plate number. Our valet attendants then get an updated list of guest names each evening with complete vehicle descriptions."

"Another one of our Standards is that all guests are to be personally escorted to a private table upon arrival. They aren't required to wait in lines or fill out any tedious paperwork. Instead, they are immediately greeted by our wine steward and offered a complimentary bottle of wine."

"By the time their wine has been poured, a fresh plate of hors d'oeuvre should arrive at their table which the kitchen began working on when the valet attendant radioed them once he identified their car," Terry continued.

"Standards tell you two things, what you need to do and how well you need to do it. They not only describe the task, but give you a way of measuring it. It's really that simple"

Chuck stopped writing, he wasn't sure he

understood.

Terry sensed this. "The tricky thing about Standards is that they are hard to recognize at first. We all have them and we let them guide our actions, but we don't naturally think in terms of Standards.

Instead, we say and think things like, 'This is just how I do things' or 'That's the way it should be done' or 'I always make sure to treat my clients with the utmost respect'."

Terry's words resonated with Chuck. He could hear himself making these kinds of statements on a regular basis. "That sounds like me," he stated.

"In order to master this 'S' of Branding, you must take these unspoken standards and externalize them by writing them down. It doesn't matter if you work by yourself or if you have 1,000 employees, if you want to create a powerful Brand, you must have clearly articulated and recorded Standards."

Terry paused to allow Chuck to continue to document his thoughts. The fire popped and hissed as they sat in silence for a few moments.

When Chuck looked up, Terry was ready for the next lesson. "Let's take a walk," he suggested.

Chuck's legs were begging to be stretched so he

agreed.

As they walked, Terry continued. "As important as Standards are, they're relatively empty without the first 'S' which is Skills. It doesn't do any good to talk about what you are going to do if you aren't able to deliver results."

"Think of it this way. If your Standards are your 'talk', then your Skills are your 'walk'. Your Skills are what makes things happen. The question you have to ask yourself is, what do I need to tangibly be able to do to deliver my standards."

Terry stopped in front of a door marked, 'Champion's Only'. "Would you like to see the back of the house?" he asked.

"Sure," Chuck replied.

"I assume 'Champion's Only' means 'Employee's Only', but what is the significance of using that kind of language," Chuck asked.

"Great question," Terry stated. "The word 'Champion' means 'one who fights for a cause'. Here at the Salebra House our guests are our cause and we fight for them. Thus, by definition, we are Champions. By acknowledging this it gives all that we do a higher purpose."

As they stepped through the door they were greeted by bright light, white walls, and the buzz of roughly 25 staff members. Some pushed carts with room service orders, others folded linens, and still others sat in front of a long row of house phones speaking with guests.

"Pretty intense, isn't it?" Terry said as he made a statement in question form.

As Chuck looked on, Terry continued, "The concept of Skill is very straightforward. Every Standard must have a Skill associated with it. In turn, you must train yourself and your staff to execute these Skills to the level which the Standard demands. Training and measurement are required to ensure that your Skills are where they need to be."

"Before we go, there is someone I want you to meet," Terry stated. As Chuck looked up he saw a short, brown haired woman approaching them.

"Mr. Stevens, it's an honor to meet you," the woman said. "I'm Grace, Grace De Lamarliere. How has your stay been so far?"

Her sparkling smile was as disarming as her soothing French accent.

"It's been unbelievable. Simply unbelievable," Chuck asserted. "Everything just seems so perfect."

Terry jumped in, "As you may recall from the invitation you received, Grace is our Director of Guest Experiences. It is her job to continually measure the quality of our product and train our Champion staff to execute the Skills required to deliver our Standards. I call her our Skill Champion."

Terry turned to Grace, "Grace, what is it that you always say about the first two 'S's?"

With almost poetic prose Grace provided her answer, "Your Skills are inconsistent at best unless you regularly measure them using your Standards. Your Standards aren't effective measuring devices unless you actually document them."

"And, there you have it," said Terry, "How about lunch?"

"Sure," replied Chuck as he finished noting Grace's response in his journal.

Terry and Chuck seated themselves at a table on the far side of the great hall that Chuck and Glori had dined in the night before. As streams of sunlight poured through the large windows, Chuck could see for the first time that this large, open room was loosely divided into three sections. A casual dining area greeted guests as they arrived at one end. The middle portion of the room was filled with comfortable looking chairs and couches that surrounded a large stone fireplace.

The last section, in which they were being served lunch, was a formal dining room that was beautifully adorned with cream and red accents. These warm colors perfectly complimented the cool aged grey of the roughhewn timbers that crisscrossed the walls and ceiling. The simplistic elegance had a calming and therapeutic effect.

Terry's crisp words broke the silence, "Do you remember the number one goal of Branding?"

Chuck quickly checked his notes to confirm his hunch, "Differentiation," he stated.

"Yes, that's it, Terry said. "And since Standards and Skills have such a transformative effect on your Brand, they go a very long way in differentiating you from your competition. But, there is one last 'S', Style."

Just as Terry finished his statement, their food arrived. Both plates seemed to contain the same dish, but the appearance of Chuck's was markedly different. His meal felt more like a work of art than something intended for human consumption.

At the center of his plate was a light pink, salmon steak adorned with dark diamond shaped grill marks.

Steamed seasonal vegetables which were oriented in a horseshoe shape around the salmon formed a brilliant rainbow of color.

To top things off, a demi glaze that had been drizzled across the salmon steak seemed to sparkle and dance in the sunlight. A perfectly apportioned garnishment of minced cilantro and mango was not only visually appealing but beckoned Chuck to begin his meal immediately.

As he picked up his fork he looked across to compare his plate to Terry's. Terry had the same salmon steak, but its placement on the side of the plate seemed to be almost accidental. Vegetables were haphazardly distributed on top of and around the salmon. The glaze and garnishment were present, but hardly held the same appeal.

As Chuck looked up his puzzled eyes met directly with Terry's.

Terry's eyes twinkled with excitement as he spoke, "If Standards represent your recipe and Skills represent the cook's ability to prepare the recipe, then Style represents the presentation of the entrée when it is served."

"In some cases it may be possible for your

competition to overlap some of your Skills and Standards, Terry continued. "However, your Style multiplies all the differences that do exist and it is your Style that truly sets you apart."

"Skills and Standards are absolutely essential and they make up the substance of your Brand. But, if your Style doesn't communicate the right message then no one will ever care to know how good your Standards and Skills actually are."

"In order to send the right message to consumers, all elements of your style have to be congruent, that is, each element needs to fit together harmoniously. Your customers will spot incongruent Style a mile away and most of the time they do this unconsciously."

"Look at this plate of food in front of me. Does it fit? Is it congruent with the Style that surrounds you?" Terry asked.

"Absolutely not," replied Chuck. "Not even close"

"Exactly," said Terry. "You knew that it didn't fit the moment you saw it."

"The first question you must ask yourself about your Style is, 'Does it accurately reflect my Standards and Skills?' Next you must ask, "Do all elements of my style fit, are they congruent?"

"It's important to note the your Style is reflected in everything from the way you answer the phone to the structure of your written communication, the layout and content of your webpage, the manner in which you dress, the way you describe your products, and even the name of your business."

"Earlier you asked about the meaning of the name we chose for our property," Terry commented.

Chuck nodded to confirm Terry's statement.

"Stand up," Terry urged him. "Look out the window and down into the valley."

As Chuck did so, he was reminded of flying in an airplane. Beneath him was a sea of clouds. The tops of the foothills far below almost looked like tiny stepping stones. The Salebra House itself, which was positioned on a jutted point, seemed to be floating in the clouds.

"In Latin, the word Salebra means 'in the clouds' and, thus, the name of our property literally means, 'The House in the Clouds'," Terry shared. "Can you think of a better place for a guest to come to renew and rejuvenate than in the heavens themselves?"

"However, this is about more than a catchy name," Terry added. "It's about accurately communicating your Skills and Standards with a Style that fits. The name

Salebra House does that for us."

Driving home, Terry's word's echoed in Chuck's mind. He could still hear Terry's saying, "It is a shame to see a company with strong Skills and Standards turn customers off with an absent or incongruent Style. But it is far worse to see a company with impeccable Style and no Skills or Standards to back it up."

If Glori had been harboring any skepticism about the Freedom Challenge, now she was a full believer.

On Chuck's end of things he was getting more out the experience than he could have anticipated. But he wasn't ready to admit that he was a full believer yet. Still, his mind was racing with ideas for his own business and he couldn't wait to get home to write them down in his journal.

## Meeting with Terry

Lessons Learned:

1. The #1 goal of Branding is Differentiation.

I need to use my Brand to make myself different so I have no competition at all.

2. There is a special formula for differentiation called the three S s of the Brand Principle.

Leverage

People — Hub — Brand

C C C

S S S

3. 1st S = Skills

My skills are inconsistent at best if I dont practice and measure them

Use my **Standards** to measure!

4. 2nd S = Standards

I cant use my Standards to measure my Skills unless I write them down.

Document, document, document!

5. 3rd S = Style
My presentation ultimately makes me different.

Is it congruent? Does it fit? Does it match my Skills & Standards?

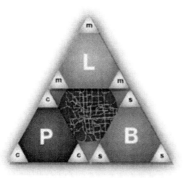

## CHAPTER EIGHT

Sitting in the back of his state's civic auditorium, Chuck was perched high above a bobbing sea of blue, red, and white. As a local marching band played a patriotic tune, the crowd waved hand-held signs and chanted in support of the out-of-state governor who was soon to take the podium.

Under ordinary circumstances Chuck was not one to get too involved in politics. When elections came around he always voted, but he didn't invest much in them outside of reading the local voter's pamphlet and casting his ballot. He had certainly never been to a campaign rally before, let alone a Presidential one.

The air around him was electric and every man, woman, and child seemed to be caught up in the frenzied energy of the evening. He'd chosen a seat in the back, in part, so that he could take in a full view of the experience and, in part, to escape from the throbbing crowd below him.

Of course, he hadn't come for the rally itself. The event was a means to an end. His instructions were to make his way to Room 120A immediately following the candidates closing remarks. Once there, he was to meet one-on-one with the 'greatest political strategist of our time' as Guy had put it.

"Mitch McAllister is the most influential person that you've never heard of," Guy had told Chuck earlier that week. "Mitch was solely responsible for the election of three of our last five Presidents. There is no greater political mastermind that exists today. An hour with Mitch is the equivalent of a combined PhD in Competitive Strategy and Resource Optimization."

As the night progressed several prominent national figures took the stage. Some were senators and others were well known actors or celebrities. Each impassioned speech was separated by a lively musical performance. Surprisingly, at the end, the candidate only addressed the crowd for fifteen brief minutes.

Still, Chuck was enchanted. He felt as though he

were watching a well-directed movie. Despite his detachment from politics, it took a concerted effort to resist the powerful, almost gravitational, forces inside him that were generated by the event.

At the conclusion of the evening, the crowd was slow to disperse and Chuck had a difficult time making his way down from the stands. More than once he was bumped and jostled by a jubilant, but inattentive participant.

Finally, he arrived at a security checkpoint manned by two uniformed officers. Neither looked particularly eager to help him. After providing his name and stating the location of his scheduled meeting, he was instructed to take a seat in one of two folding chairs that were located nearby.

After waiting at least five minutes, Chuck was summoned by one of the officers and escorted down a long corridor to Room 120A.

The officer held the door open and motioned for Chuck to enter. Once inside, Chuck discovered that the room was empty. He turned to the officer with a puzzled look on his face.

"I'm sure your party will be here to meet with you shortly," the officer said lethargically and turned to leave.

Just as the latch was about to touch the strike plate, the door began to swing open again. Assuming that this marked the arrival of his guest, Chuck rose to greet him.

To his surprise, Chuck was greeted by a sharply dressed woman in her early fifties.

"Are you Chuck Stevens?" the woman asked as she offered her hand.

"Yes, I am," Chuck answered. "I believe I'm here to meet with Mitch McAllister?"

"Good," the woman replied. "Then we're both in the right place."

As she gestured toward a set of chairs nearby, she continued, "Let's get started, I've only got about sixty minutes before we fly out for our next campaign stop."

Chuck hesitated for a moment and then followed her lead. "You're Mitch McAllister?" he confirmed.

"Yes, I am," Mitch responded. "I was named after my grandfather who died in World War II. My parents had five girls and, being the youngest, I was their last hope for a son. The official name on my birth certificate is Michelle, but no one ever uses it. Even my husband refers to me as Mitch."

"I take it you were expecting a man," Mitch added

quickly.

"I guess I was," Chuck admitted. "I bet your name can make things a little tricky given your line of work."

"Actually, my name is a huge advantage," Mitch replied. "I frequently leverage it to create a memorable position for myself in people's minds before I meet them. But, I don't want to get ahead myself. That's part of what I wanted to share with you tonight."

"Ok, so where do we start?" asked Chuck as he leaned over to retrieve his journal from his briefcase. As always, he was eager get things going.

"Good question," said Mitch. "Tell me, what do you know about running a political campaign?"

"Not a whole lot," Chuck confessed. "Honestly, I try to stay away from politics. When I do think of campaigns, I think of a bunch of signs all over town that all seem to say the same thing. Even the candidates themselves seem to repeat the same mantra: I can do it better than the other guy, my way is the best, and I'll work harder."

"Well said," Mitch commented with a chuckle. "You nailed it for sure."

She paused for a moment and then added, "The sad thing is that your sentiments could easily describe the presence that most real estate agents have in their communities."

This was a sobering thought, but Chuck knew that it was true. He took a moment to let it sink in.

"I do agree with you," Chuck replied. "But, I guess I'll have to watch what I say from now on. I didn't anticipate that you'd turn my statement around and use it against me."

"That's politics," Mitch said with a twinkle in her eye. "But I do promise I'll play fair from here on out."

"On a serious note, I want to point out that the game of politics has changed a lot in the last few decades," Mitch continued. "Most of these changes can be summarized with one word: Leverage."

"Leverage applies to much more that politics, but before I continue I'd like to tell you how I first learned about Leverage." Mitch stated.

"When I was girl, my father worked for the director of the National Parks Service and he led a special team that was commissioned by the Mission '66 initiative to renovate and upgrade many of our country's National Parks during the late 1950's and early 1960's. He traveled quite a bit during that time and my sisters and I rarely got to see him."

"One summer we took a family vacation to one of the parks my father's team was working on. It was a trip I'll never forget. We stayed in a newly built visitor's center that was nestled between several alpine lakes and that lay in the shadow of a rugged mountain."

"For several weeks we ran and played in the streams and meadows, picked flowers, and collected bugs of every shape and size. Toward the end of our stay, my father took us on a long hike. As we walked along the park's newly constructed trails we came across a work party. They were cleaning up a large rockslide that had made the path impassable just a few days earlier."

"My father explained that it would have taken several weeks to bring in machinery to take care of the slide so instead the workers were moving the rocks by hand. Along with my sisters, I watched in fascination as these men literally moved boulders that were taller than they were. Instead of trying to push or pull them, these men worked together using heavy steel bars and smaller rocks to slowly roll the boulders."

"By placing the steel rods at the base of these boulders, and pulling downward, the workers used the power of leverage to inch the rocks forward until they picked up momentum. This required only a fraction of the effort that would have otherwise been required and allowed the workers to complete the entire task in less than a week."

Chuck was lost in Mitch's story. Minutes earlier he had stopped writing and could now see himself standing on a mountain path surrounded by boulders. As a gust of wind whipped across his face, he could clearly hear the sound of steel bars clanking and the men as they shouted back and forth to each other.

All of a sudden Chuck realized that everything around him had gone silent and his mind quickly transported him back to Room 120A. It was only then that he consciously noticed that Mitch had stopped talking.

When Chuck looked up he noticed that Mitch had a playful gleam in her eyes. Slowly she leaned toward him and spoke in a muted tone.

"The secret to my success has little to do with the fact that I actually use Leverage. Any decent campaign strategist uses Leverage these days. My success has much more to do with the special ways in which I use Leverage."

"There is a specific formula for Leverage that I use with all the campaigns I manage. The formula is:

Memorability, Minutes, and Money. I call them the three 'M's of the Leverage Principle."

Just as Mitch was about to begin explaining her formula the door to Room 120A opened and one of Mitch's campaign aides walked through the doorway. The young man, dressed in khaki slacks and a tie, looked as though he had barely graduated from high school.

"Ms. McAllister, ma'am, we've got a little situation," the young man began before he stopped short, staring at Mitch and Chuck. "I'm terribly sorry ma'am," he continued, "I thought you were alone."

"Look," he stammered, "I've got to talk to you about something."

Chuck thought he detected a knowing look of sympathy on Mitch's face as she regarded her troubled assistant. "Sure Jaime, just give me moment," Mitch replied.

With a nod, Jaime turned and left the room.

"This shouldn't take more than a minute," Mitch said as she gestured toward the door. "Do you mind?"

As Chuck shook his head, Mitch rose and exited the room.

When she returned, Mitch had a big smile on her face and made a clucking sound with her mouth.

"When you're a rookie everything seems like an emergency," Mitch commented as she slid back into her chair.

Noting the curious look on Chuck's face, Mitch decided to fill him in on her conversation with Jaime.

"Jaime is a college intern and he's been with us about six months. As you can imagine, I keep him very busy. One of his jobs is to coordinate with the media to set up interviews and to manage requests for our campaign to make official comments about different issues."

"The concern Jaime had tonight was about an issue that a reporter had asked our campaign to comment on. Given the recent news headlines, this issue has become somewhat inflammatory. Jaime's specific concern was that making a comment would force us to pick a side..."

As Mitch paused, Chuck looked up at her trying to interpret the odd smile on her face.

Mitch shook her head playfully, "You should have seen the look on his face when I told him that we actually wanted to take a side."

"You see, Chuck," Mitch continued, "this fits perfectly with the first Leverage concept that I wanted to share with you, the concept of Memorability."

"In days of old, politicians were careful not to take

sides and tried to appeal to everybody. They didn't want to say anything that would alienate them from the mass of voters."

"However, things are different today. Nearly 80 to 90 percent of voters have firmly staked a claim on one side of the partisan fence and have made up their mind about who they will vote for before the first campaign sign is ever posted. This means that most political races are actually determined by 10 to 20 percent of the population which is made up of independent voters who can be swayed one way or another."

"The key to winning these independent votes begins with determining the top two or three issues that the voters in this influential 10 to 20 percent minority consider the most important."

"Next, a candidate must build his or her policy platform around the desirable side of these issues, even if this means rubbing some traditional partisan voters the wrong way. It is always tempting to play a tune that pleases the majority, but it is consistently more effective to connect directly with the influential minority. "

"Finally, candidates must communicate with these independent voters in a manner that polarizes their competition on the opposite side of these same issues."

"When a candidate does all this successfully, the byproduct is that he or she creates a unique, desirable, and memorable position in voters' minds."

"A position that, if constructed effectively, other competing candidates cannot ever hope to occupy. Most importantly, this exclusive and memorable position in the minds of voters inevitably translates into success on election day."

While Mitch had been lecturing, Chuck had been scribbling furiously in his journal. Mitch paused to allow him to catch up. When Chuck was finished, he looked up to let Mitch know he was ready for her to continue.

"Memorability is always an essential part of a campaign, but there are two more 'M's," Mitch shared. "These are especially important to identify when a candidate is facing a truly formidable opponent."

"The second 'M' is the concept of Minutes and it has to do with how you spend your time," Mitch continued.

"To leverage Minutes, a campaign must also focus a majority of its time on the same 10 to 20 percent of independent voters that it targets with its policy platform."

Chuck flipped a page in his journal and resumed his note taking as Mitch continued.

"Major political candidates get offers to make appearances across the country to a wide variety of groups. Opportunities literally crop up all over the place."

"The temptation, even with a focused and Memorable policy platform, is to try to do it all."

Mitch paused again, as though searching for a thought. "I guess the reason that this temptation is so strong is that it feels like the candidate is missing a big opportunity each time he or she says no to an appearance or event."

"The funny thing is that the fear of loss often has a stronger pull than rational thought. This is why so many promising candidates fade as an election nears. The fear of losing an opportunity drives them to dilute their focus and they stop leveraging their Minutes."

"My rule for the concept of Minutes is that 80% of our campaign time must be focused on events, and with groups, that are strongly associated with the same independent voters for whom we've crafted our policy platform."

In a way, Chuck could identify with the fear of loss that Mitch had referenced. It's not that he was actually afraid of losing to another agent, but he just couldn't stand to pass up an opportunity even if it didn't seem to fit with his overall business plan. He felt like he could literally see the dollars passing through his hands if he didn't pull the trigger.

For the second time in the evening Chuck realized that his thoughts had wandered and that Mitch had stopped talking. Chuck looked down at his notes and then upward to meet Mitch's gaze. It was almost as though she knew his thoughts.

"There is a powerful myth I'd like to dispel and it has to do with final "M", the concept of Money."

"A lot of candidates and campaign managers think that with enough money they can win any race or that more money can resurrect a floundering campaign."

"Nothing could be further from the truth," Mitch stated.

As Mitch was about to begin her next sentence the mobile smart phone sitting on the desk in front of her rang with a peculiar musical sound.

"I'm sorry about all the interruptions Chuck, but this is an urgent call," Mitch apologized.

The conversation on Mitch's end consisted of a series of 'yeses' and 'oks' and it concluded with a 'will do".

"Chuck, do you mind taking a walk with me?' Mitch

asked when she finished.

All though he was somewhat surprised by the request given the circumstances, he nodded and gathered his belongings.

As Chuck and Mitch made their way down the hallway leading away from Room 120A Mitch explained, "Our pilot has been tracking a storm that is moving across the state. She wants to leave now so that we can get over the mountains before it hits."

"Chuck, as I was saying, the belief that money can solve all problems, especially political or business related problems, is dangerously false."

"When money is abundant it is often unwisely spent in a whole variety of ways. This is especially true with inexperienced campaign directors and candidates."

"In contrast, when money is short, it creates a valuable educational opportunity. If they are to be successful, campaign directors and candidates must learn how to allocate a limited supply of money in a manner that provides the highest possible return on investment."

"This is the foundation of the Leverage concept of Money, return on investment. With respect to Money, the most critical indicator of a campaign's potential success is not the quantity of money it has, but how it is spent and the return on investment it earns."

"Practically speaking, I run very lean campaigns and I keep my overhead costs well below the donation revenue that we receive each month. This frees up as much money as possible for outreach," Mitch continued.

"In order to maximize the return on investment for our outreach dollars, I ask three simple questions every time I spend money in this area."

"First, I ask whether the impact on our target group of independent voters will be positive, neutral, or negative."

"Second, I ask if there is anything else that is similar to invest our money in that could have an even greater positive impact on our target group."

"Finally, I ask what the impact or negative cost would be if we didn't spend the money."

"If spending money in the proposed way will have a direct and positive impact on our target group of independent voters, if there are no other similar alternatives that will have a greater positive impact, and the cost of missing the opportunity is higher than the positive impact the expense will have, then I know we are effectively leveraging our money."

Just as Mitch had finished her last statement they

exited the building via a set of doors that were held open by yet another pair of security guards.

As they did so, the sound that greeted Mitch and Chuck's ears was thunderous. The helicopter in front of them not only generated an incredible amount of noise, but the strong airflow nearly blew Chuck's journal from his hands.

To compensate for the rhythmic chopping of the helicopter's rotors, Mitch leaned close to Chuck's ear to finish her lesson.

"Chuck, there is one final thing I need to tell you about Leverage. Now that you understand the concepts of Memorability, Minutes, and Money, it is important that you also understand the power of compound Leverage."

"When the decisions you make regarding Money reinforce the decisions you already made about Minutes and Memorability then you begin multiplying the effect of each piece of Leverage."

"Let me give you an example. Do you see the helicopter in front of us?"

Although Chuck thought it was a ridiculous question given the proximity of the aircraft, he gave a quick nod.

"The cost of renting a helicopter to get back and forth

to airports is greater than the cost of a Town Car or limousine. However, it ends up generating a strong return on investment because it gives our campaign a greater number of opportunities to get in front of our target group over time. This is Money Leverage."

"Now, when our Money Leverage is aligned with the target group that we want to spend our Minutes in front of, and the target group with which we want to build our Memorability, each one of these individual leverage points acts on the others so that the total leveraged effect is greater than the sum of the effect of the individual leverage points."

"When we leverage our Money, we get more Minutes, and we can use these additional Minutes to create more Memorability. In turn, more Money is generated via donation dollars. This is the power of compound Leverage," Mitch declared triumphantly.

"Just like moving a boulder, it would be impossible to run a political campaign in today's environment without Leverage." Mitch continued.

"If you try to address every possible issue and appeal to everybody, if you spend your time chasing every opportunity, or if you spread your money across a wide variety of expenses, it's like trying to push a boulder with just your hands. You're not going to get very far that way."

"But, if you focus on a small group of voters and leverage a few key issues, if you selectively allocate your time to key opportunities, and you focus on return on investment when you spend your money, you create a dynamic that functions just like the steel bars that allow workers to move boulders with ease."

"That's it Chuck, I've got to get going," Mitch said as she offered her hand.

With that, Mitch was off.  As a guard opened the door for her to board the helicopter, Chuck could see Mitch's entire team and the candidate waiting for her.

Chuck had never been this close to a helicopter before and, now that he had grown accustomed to it, the lights and sounds were almost hypnotizing. He stood and watched as the helicopter lifted effortlessly into the night sky.

While his eyes followed the flashing lights into the distance, Chuck began to consider how the three 'M's of Leverage, Memorability, Minutes, and Money, applied to his business and how he could create compound Leverage. A raindrop that landed in the middle of Chuck's face interrupted his thoughts and he quickly made his way to his car.

By the time he reached it, the rain was falling steadily. Chuck took a few minutes, as raindrops pelted his windshield, to add a few final thoughts to his journal before he drove home for the evening.

# Meeting with Mitch

Lessons Learned:

1. Leverage creates momentum and requires less energy.

   How I use Leverage is just as important as the fact that I use it.

2. There is a special formula called the three M.s of the Leverage Principle.

M ── Leverage ── M

M

(Hub)

People ──── Brand

C   C        S   S

3. 1st M = Memorability

I need to select one thing that
makes me different and create
a unique and desireable position
out of it.

Focus on the few, not the many!

4. 2nd M = Minutes

The temptation is to try to do
it all and Fear of lost
opportunity can dilute my focus.

Focus 80% of my time on the
people and things that matter!

5. 3rd M = Money

Not how much I spend, but
what is my return on investment.

Will the money I spend have a direct impact on growing my business? i.e. is it focused in or around my Hub?

6. Compound Leverage = Using Memorability, Minutes, & Money at the same time in and around my Hub.

Dont try to push a boulder with your hands!

Use Leverage!

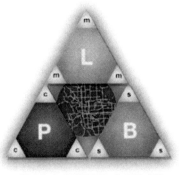

# CHAPTER **NINE**

**A**s Chuck walked toward the modern looking front entrance of Grayson Middle School his mind began to wander. Several weeks had passed since the night of the campaign rally and Chuck had not yet heard from Guy regarding his final coaching session.

For the first week or so he'd actually been relieved because there was so much other work to be done. Even with his assistant back from her honeymoon things seemed as hectic as they ever had been.

Still, in between the many meetings, tasks, and phone calls that filled his days, his mind often drifted to his interactions with the Coach, Terry Jacobs, and Mitch McAllister. It puzzled him, and at times irritated him, that Guy had not contacted him to bring closure to this whole experience.

In some ways Chuck felt like the lessons he had learned had truly changed both him and his business. Yet, in other ways, he felt like the same old Chuck running the same old business.

It wasn't a matter of not understanding the three Principles. Chuck's challenge with the material had more to do with implementation. "How am I supposed to make these fundamental changes in my business while I'm still running it day-to-day?" Chuck frequently asked himself.

In the absence of a compelling answer to his question, Chuck had attempted to do the best he could. Practically speaking, this meant he returned to business as usual, albeit with a few key enhancements.

If nothing else, the Freedom Challenge seemed to have given Chuck new found energy and, because of it, he had increased the intensity with which he approached each day.

One promise he made to himself was that he was going to stop limiting the time spent with his family to that which was left over at the end of each day. Frankly, adjusting his schedule to account for this shift in priorities had been his greatest challenge. Nonetheless, he was determined to keep his commitment.

As chance would have it, this was the very reason he was about to enter his son's school. A few weeks ago Glori had mentioned that Grayson Middle School was looking for parent volunteers to help out with their annual field day and suggested that Chuck sign up.

Amy, his assistant, had contacted the school's secretary and relayed a message back to Chuck that he was to meet the head P.E. teacher out on the track at 9:30 am after checking in at the front office.

Just as Chuck reached for the handle of the school's front door, it began to open from the inside. Seeing the silhouette of another person on the other side of the glass door, Chuck quickly stepped to the right to allow the other party to exit. To his surprise, no one walked through the door. When he peered inside he came face-to-face with a smiling Guy Chamberlin.

"Come on in, Chuck," Guy exclaimed.

There was something about his interactions with Guy that always seemed to put Chuck at a loss for words. However, he quickly recovered.

"Thanks Guy," Chuck replied. "I was beginning to think you had forgotten about me."

"Good," Guy answered. "Then my timing is perfect."

As they walked to the front office Guy explained that

giving Chuck ample time to think about and to try to implement the concepts he had learned was a critical part of the Challenge. Guy also confessed that he and Glori had conspired to influence Chuck into signing up as a field day volunteer.

"Good Morning, Alice," Guy said as he and Chuck entered the office.

"Good Morning, Mr. Chamberlin," Alice responded. "And the same to you Mr. Stevens."

Chuck had never met Alice, the school secretary, but Glori spoke quite highly of her. For a moment he wondered how Alice recognized him, but then he remembered to never second guess anything when he was with Guy.

"Mr. Stevens, I trust that Mr. Chamberlin has told you about your reassignment," Alice continued.

"Not yet, Alice, but thank you for all your help," Guy jumped in.

As Chuck filled out the required waivers, Guy explained that the two of them would be volunteering to help supervise the inside game room rather than being out on the field. Secretly, Chuck wondered what Guy had up his sleeve.

Guy led the way as he and Chuck made their way

down a long linoleum lined hallway. Finally, Guy stopped in front of a classroom and gestured toward the door.

The two entered the room to find a subdued, but engaged group of 6th, 7th, and 8th grade students playing dominoes, cards, and various board games.

Guy walked Chuck over to a table where six kids were playing what looked like a half-finished game of Risk.

"I used to love this game as a kid," Chuck said with a smile that suggested he was picturing memories from his past. "If I remember correctly, we talked a little about Risk in our first meeting?"

"Perhaps we did. Let's sit and watch them play a little," Guy suggested with a playful expression that told Chuck it was no accident that these students were playing Risk.

The two men sat on the edge of a nearby table as they watched the kids gasp in dismay and chant in delight as each role of the dice was made. Some of them kept a straight face in an attempt to bluff their competitors. Others openly teased their rivals as they positioned their game pieces on the board.

More importantly, Chuck and Guy could feel that the

students were genuinely having fun and that there was a certain intensity surrounding the game. After a few more strategic moves were made, Guy motioned Chuck over to a whiteboard in a quiet corner of the room.

"Let me tie everything together for you, Chuck," he said. Then Guy began to draw a large diagram on the whiteboard. It consisted of a large triangle made up of smaller triangles and a circle in the center.

As Guy added labels to triangles and the circle, Chuck immediately recognized the Freedom Formula that Guy had outlined in their first coaching session and that he had learned about in detail from each of Guy's subject matter experts.

First, there was the Primary Hub in the middle. Next, there were the 3 'C's of the People Principle: Contribution, Communication, and Connection. These were followed by the 3 'S's of the Brand Principle: Skills, Standards, and Style. Finally, there were the 3 'M's of the Leverage Principle: Memorability, Minutes, and Money.

"Chuck," Guy began, "I've got a question for you. What's missing from the lesson?"

The answer came surprisingly easy to Chuck. "Implementation," he quickly replied.

"Exactly," Guy exclaimed. "So far you've learned

about the Freedom Challenge and the concepts associated with it, but I haven't shown you how to take action. There has to be a vehicle for implementation."

"For a moment, let's consider something like the game of Risk as a potential vehicle," Guy suggested. "Where does the game of Risk take place?"

"On a game board?" Chuck replied, slightly unsure of his answer.

"Yes. And that's important because studies show that the brain works better when there are defined boundaries or a specific context on which to focus. But what is on the board?" Guy asked.

"A map," Chuck responded.

"Good," Guy continued. "How is the map divided?"

"By countries," Chuck responded.

"Correct," Guy stated. "Now, let me tell you how the game of Risk and the Freedom Challenge are alike."

Chuck watch as Guy grabbed a small cardboard tube next to the whiteboard and withdrew a large, laminated map. Once it was unrolled Guy used several push pins to attach it to the wall next to the whiteboard. All in all it was as tall as the whiteboard and about half as wide.

Upon closer examination, Chuck found that it was a map of a small, but well-to-do neighborhood in Reed

County. However, the map was unlike any he had seen. Instead of being made out of a single piece of paper it appeared to be constructed out of multiple plat maps that had been copied from county records and pasted together.

As Chuck turned toward him with a quizzical look Guy gestured back toward the map and continued with his lesson.

"This is the map I used when I first accepted the Freedom Challenge decades ago," Guy confessed. "It took me a lot of time to create it, but today you can print maps like this off the internet very easily."

"Just as in the game of Risk, a map will be your game board. However, your map will only include the 1000 homes contained in your Primary Hub and it will be divided into parcels like my map is rather than the countries you see on a Risk game board."

"I've got another question for you Chuck," Guy stated. "How is the game of Risk played?"

"Well, it's pretty simple actually," Chuck replied. "Players take turns drawing cards and strategically placing game pieces on the board."

"When two players go head-to-head they role dice to determine the victor; the number of dice they get to role depends on how well they've laid out their game pieces."

"The goal is world domination. Ultimately the outcome of the game is determined by a combination of skill and luck."

"Well said Chuck, well said," Guy commented. "So which has a greater impact on the outcome of the game, skill or luck?"

"Skill," said Chuck with confidence. "Those that truly understand the game and think through their moves in advance will always come out on top; even if they have to adjust to a run of bad luck."

"And so it is with the Freedom Challenge," Guy shared.

"The difference is that you don't have to wait to draw the right card when you're playing the game that goes along with the Freedom Challenge. When it comes to your actions, you control your own destiny; you decide what moves you want to make and when you make them," Guy shared.

"And," Guy paused as if he were about to make an important point. "The better your strategy, which is simply the coordination of all your actions, the less vulnerable you will be to luck when you go head-to-head with other agents."

Chuck's mind began to wander as Guy's last sentence trailed off. The analogy Guy had drawn made perfect sense to him. But, he still didn't see a clear path for implementation.

His thoughts were soon interrupted by the sound of red and black push pins spilling out of a small plastic container onto the table in front of him.

"Chuck, tell me the goal of the game of Risk again," Guy requested.

"World domination," Chuck replied.

"Precisely," Guy said. "That is the same goal of the Freedom Challenge, domination within your Primary Hub."

"Primary Hub domination is measured by your market share percentage," Guy continued. "Each time you take a listing within your Primary Hub put a red push pin on that parcel. If one of your competitors takes a listing in your Primary Hub put a black push pin on that parcel."

"When you have listed 50% or more of the houses for sale in your Primary Hub you've reached a level of achievement that can be considered domination," Guy stated.

Just as Guy finished his last sentence, Chuck held up

a hand for him to stop.

"Excuse me for interrupting Guy. The comparison you are making to the game of Risk makes a lot of sense to me and I can now see why the concept of the Primary Hub is so important to the Freedom Formula," Chuck said.

"But all this talk about red pins and black pins and going head-to-head against other agents to compete for listings sounds a lot like the part of Risk where players roll dice to determine who wins a confrontation."

"What about the part of the game where players draw cards and lay out their armies before they go head-to-head in a confrontation?" Chuck asked.

"I'm glad you asked, Chuck," Guy said.

"As a game, the Freedom Challenge includes a myriad of marketing activities that you select from each week. Each individual activity has a point value assigned to it," Guy continued.

"In the same way that you combine different cards in the game of Risk to make moves, you combine marketing activities within your Primary Hub to make moves in the Freedom Challenge."

"Your weekly goal is to score at least 2000 points with the moves you make. When you accrue 2000 points or more each week you can be sure that you are taking the actions necessary to dominate within your Primary Hub."

As Guy spoke Chuck found himself nodding in agreement. His previous doubts about a concentrated strategy like geographic farming were being replaced by the robust strategies of the Freedom Challenge.

Chuck listened as Guy continued to share how Chuck could grow his market share by 50% in 12 months by simply playing the game that had been laid out in front of him. Chuck's head began to swim. All of a sudden it was becoming clear. All the books he had read and all the seminars he had attended were being stacked one on top of the other as Guy masterfully explained how to play the Freedom Challenge.

In one moment Guy was outlining a detailed plan for using open houses to increase his listings and the next he was talking about organizing philanthropic programs within the community. Guy covered dozens of activities including door knocking, business-to-business strategies, and direct mail methods.

He even surprised Chuck when he spoke of the internet, creating custom landing pages, and the use of garage sale systems. What seemed to stand out most was how Guy had created a comprehensive strategy out of all these methods. He had never seen an agent work this way. Most of the top producers he knew simply worked hard for their clients and gave great customer service.

Guy could see Chuck beginning to glaze over and pulled him back. "I call this 'layering', Chuck. Good strategy doesn't always mean inventing something new. It can also entail moving things around so they fit better together. Have you ever heard the saying, 'The whole is greater than the sum of its parts'?"

"Yes," Chuck answered.

"Well the same is true in the Freedom Challenge. I've updated a few things since I took the Challenge years ago. My focus has been taking the most successful marketing activities I could find and 'layering' them one on top of another."

"Makes sense," said Chuck.

"It should," Guy stated in a matter-of-fact tone. "Because it works."

"In fact, from what I've seen, and I've seen a lot Chuck, it is the most effective way to build a real estate business," Guy continued.

"Ok," said Chuck. "Let me see if I've got it."

"First, I start with the 1000 homes in my Primary

Hub, using the criteria you mentioned in our first meeting, to determine the right Hub." Chuck began.

"Next, I build a game board by assembling a big map with detail down to the parcel level of that Hub," he continued.

"So far so good," Guy affirmed.

"Then, I begin playing the game by choosing…," Chuck paused for a moment. "I'm mean by 'layering' marketing activities within my Primary Hub in order to score 2000 points each week."

"Good," Guy said.

"Finally, I know that I have dominant market share within my Primary Hub when my red pins out number all the other agents black pins on my map."

"Yes," Guy added. "Because having more red pins than black pins means you control at least 50 percent of the listings which is how we define dominate market share."

"Right," said Chuck. "And when I have dominate market share in my Primary Hub I'm guessing that I just continue playing the game. Can I just add a second Primary Hub?"

"Secondary Hub," Guy stated. "You'll add a Secondary Hub. In fact, you can add multiple Secondary

Hubs over time but you'll never replace your Primary Hub."

"So, are the criteria the same for Secondary Hubs?" Chuck asked.

"I'm glad you asked Chuck," Guy said. "The criteria are similar but there are some important differences."

"There are two options for Secondary Hubs. First, you can extend the borders of your Primary Hub to include an additional 1000 homes. In this case the criteria are identical to the criteria you will use for your Primary Hub."

"Your other option for a Secondary Hub is to find what I call a 'feeder' neighborhood. Think of it this way. At some point in the past the current residents of your Primary Hub moved into your Primary Hub from other neighborhoods. A single neighborhood from which the largest percentage of your current Primary Hub residents has recently moved is called a 'feeder' neighborhood because it feeds your Primary Hub with new homeowners."

"A twist on this is selecting a neighborhood that your Primary Hub feeds. That is, a single neighborhood to which the largest percentage of your Primary Hub residents has recently moved or would move given the right opportunity," Guy continued.

Chuck finally jumped in. "I think I get it," he stated. "When I list houses in a 'feeder' neighborhood that I turn into a Secondary Hub I generate buyers for the listings I already have in my Primary Hub."

"Or," Chuck continued, "I can help the sellers in my Primary Hub move up to the neighborhood my Primary Hub feeds by securing listings there and adding it as a Secondary Hub."

"I couldn't have said it better myself," Guy responded. "The important thing to remember when growing your business past your Primary Hub is the 50 percent market share rule. You can't take on another Hub until you have 50 percent of the listings in the ones you're currently working."

Guy then finished his explanation of Secondary Hubs by sharing with Chuck how the Freedom Formula and the Principles of People, Brand, and Leverage take on additional meaning when the need for employees arises. Guy outlined how to hire, train, and compensate other agents to help Chuck with his business as well as what adding each hub should realistically contribute to Chuck's bottom line.

"Wow, this is more like the game of Risk than I ever

would have guessed," Chuck confessed.

"There is just one more piece missing," Guy stated.

"There is?" Chuck asked.

"Yes," said Guy. "It has to do with the three questions that I asked you at the end of our first coaching session?"

Chuck remembered the three questions well. They were:

1. What would you do with your life if you had more than enough money and didn't need to work?
2. What would you do if you knew you couldn't fail?
3. What makes you come alive?

The night Guy had first asked him to write them down in his journal had been a sleepless one. He lay awake pondering the true purpose behind his daily actions, or the 'Higher Purpose of Business' as Guy had so eloquently put it.

For several weeks thereafter he had even wondered if he had a 'Higher Purpose'. All he really wanted to do was be successful, enjoy life, and spend time with his family.

Then one day while he was driving it hit him. Although he was in the middle of rush hour traffic, Chuck pulled his vehicle to the side of the road as quickly as he could and began writing in his journal.

What he initially guessed to be a paragraph or two of

ideas continued on page after page. When he was done he'd filled more than a dozen pages.

The act of writing out his 'Higher Purpose of Business' had made Chuck feel more alive than he had felt in years. Surprisingly, he had felt reluctant to share it with anyone, even Glori.

Now, for the first time, Chuck felt ready to discuss the topic with someone other than himself. Slowly, he opened his journal, leafed through it until he found the passage in question, and passed it to Guy.

Chuck then waited for what seemed to be an eternity as Guy carefully read every word Chuck had written about his 'Higher Purpose of Business'.

Finally, Guy's eyes lifted from the pages of the journal and connected firmly with Chuck's.

"Thank you Chuck," Guy began. "Thank you for taking these questions seriously and thank you for sharing your responses with me."

Even though Guy had finished speaking, he maintained steady eye contact with Chuck. In fact, his eyes communicated more than his words ever could have. Without setting out to do so, Chuck had earned Guy's upmost respect.

For the first time since they had met, Chuck now felt

on equal standing with Guy. Not in terms of his accomplishments, but in terms of the positive difference Chuck hoped to have on those around him.

When Guy spoke again his voice took on a deeper more serious tone. "Chuck, you have such a strong grasp of the 'Higher Purpose of Business' that there is nothing more I can teach you about it. The rest you'll have to learn as you go."

"But I do need to share with you why it is so important," Guy added.

Guy then asked Chuck, "How does it feel to win at the game of Risk?"

"Tiring," Chuck said as he joked about the length of an average game of Risk. "And exhilarating at the same time," he added.

"Yes," Guy affirmed. "But what then, what are you left with?"

Chuck took a moment to consider Guy's question. While he did so he gazed back across the room at the group of students who had been playing Risk when they entered the room. The game was now over and had been put away.

Even without the game to bring them together, the students continued to talk and laugh with each other. In fact, Chuck couldn't even tell who had won. The victory, while real, had been short lived and now appeared to be irrelevant.

"Experiences and relationships," Chuck finally answered. "You're left with the experiences you had and the relationships you built."

"Exactly," said Guy. "So you better make the experience fun and foster meaningful relationships, otherwise your victory with be an empty one."

"Without understanding and aligning your actions with your 'Higher Purpose of Business' you will burn out eventually," Guy shared.

"And when I say burn out, I mean crash and burn," Guy continued. "It's never pretty. For some people it happens when they are still in their first year of real estate and for others it's in their tenth. Regardless, the result is still the same."

"I think I understand," said Chuck. "But my 'Higher Purpose of Business' seems so far away."

"Based on where I am today, it almost seems out of reach," Chuck added.

"Yes, I'm sure it does," Guy stated. "The reason for this is that your 'Higher Purpose of Business' only becomes possible when your real estate business succeeds in a big way for a sustained period of time."

"Everything is part of a natural progression," Guy continued. "By restructuring your business according to the Freedom Formula and by playing the Freedom Challenge as a game, you'll first gain market share."

"Market share in turn will give you more profits."

"Profits, when you operate your business according to the Freedom Formula, will allow you to buy your time back."

"Ultimately, market share, profits, and time will set you free," Guy paused for emphasis, "Free to explore and live out your 'Higher Purpose of Business'."

After they wrapped up their conversation, Guy and Chuck spent the rest of the morning playing games with the Grayson Middle School students who had elected to play inside for the school's field day. Overall, the interaction reminded Chuck of how much energy he felt when he was at play.

When Chuck returned to his office later that afternoon he immediately pulled out his journal and quickly put together a plan that would allow him to begin playing the Freedom Challenge as a game the following Monday.

As Chuck leaned back in his chair to review the list

of action items he had just generated, a strange sensation passed over him. It was the realization that, for the first time in his real estate career, he actually felt equipped to reach the level of performance of which he knew he was capable.

# 2nd Meeting with Guy

Lessons Learned:

1. Just like the game of Risk.

    Game Board = Map
    Game Pieces = Pins
    Goal = Geographic Domination

2. Domination = 50% market share OR more in my Primary Hub.

Layer my marketing activities within my Hub and score at least 2000 points per week.

50% rule. I cant start another hub until I have 50% of the listings in my Hub.

This is how it works!

FREEDOM!!!

Time

Profit

Market

3rd Hub 1000    Share    2nd Hub 1000

M    Leverage    M

M

Primary Hub 1000

People    Brand

C    C    S    S

C    C    S    S

3. My Higher Purpose of Business will give my efforts meaning.

   Playing makes me feel alive and gives me energy!

4. All I will be left with at the end are the experiences I had and the relationships I made.

   So, I need to make sure I have fun and build meaningful relationships!

# I Finally See How I Can Do This!

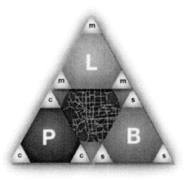

## CHAPTER **TEN**

As he pulled off Old Mountain Highway and into the parking lot of Max's BBQ, an overworked and overstressed real estate agent let out a long audible sigh.

It was nearly impossible to find a parking spot at Max's, even on a Tuesday night. Max's BBQ had taken over an old roadside diner about two decades ago and now regularly attracted business from not only Reed County, but the surrounding counties as well.

The agent was very grateful when he found a parking spot down the first aisle nearest the building. Although his car was now in park and closely nestled between two SUV's he was not yet ready to exit his vehicle.

Instead he rested his head up against the steering wheel and listened to the quiet purr of his engine. As he sat his thoughts turned to the preceding week, especially the last 48 hours.

Today was the end of an intense month wrought with difficulties and challenges. Overall, it hadn't been a bad month financially, but the stress associated with it had taken its toll.

On top of all this he had some serious questions about his business. He wasn't about to give up, but he knew that he had to make some changes.

While it was true that he had out performed many of his industry peers and that he enjoyed a strong reputation in the marketplace, there were times in which his business seemed so far out of control that it unnerved him.

To make matters worse, the demands that his business placed on him seemed to be having an increasingly negative effect on his family.

It all felt like a bad dream, one from which he hoped that he could somehow wake up. He wasn't sure what the answers were, but he knew he needed to find them. In the meantime, he also knew that he needed to eat.

Walking through the front door of Max's BBQ was like entering an anthill. The restaurant was bustling with activity. Waiters and waitresses crisscrossed as they carried heavy trays with twice the food required for the parties they were serving.

Men and women carrying bus tubs darted quickly in and out like hummingbirds as they hovered over empty tables. Patrons everywhere were talking and laughing.

Despite the chaos, the agent received a friendly greeting from one of the hostesses. Just as she was about to tell him that that he would have to wait 20 to 30 minutes for a table, Max himself strode confidently around the corner.

"Alex, I was hoping I'd see you tonight," Max exclaimed as he walked over and extended his hand. "How's business?"

As Alex shook the proprietor's hand he was struck by what a good friend the older man had become. While he was not normally one to be at a loss for words, Alex struggled to articulate a response, "Well Max, let's just say I'm in need of some comfort food tonight."

"That kind of a month, huh," Max commented. "Come this way, I've got a table ready for you."

Alex was seated no more than 30 seconds before he had a large glass of sweet tea in front of him.

"The Sampler for you Alex?" Max asked.

"Yes, please," Alex responded.

Although Alex had grown accustomed to having Max personally wait on him over the last few months, it was rather unusual for Max to work the dining room. These days Max spent most of his time greeting patrons and ensuring that their visit was all that they had hoped for.

"Coming right up," Max said. "Say, do you mind if I join you tonight. I haven't had dinner yet myself."

"Be my guest," Alex replied. "Maybe you could even help me figure some things out," he joked.

In less than 10 minutes, two Sampler platters sat in front of Alex and Max. Few words were shared between the two men as they busily started in on their meal.

"So, how's business…everything ok?" Max finally inquired with a look that told Alex he already knew what Alex was going to say.

Alex proceeded to share some of his more recent business frustrations with Max.

Max listened intently, sipped his tea, nodded, and smiled as Alex spoke.

When Alex was finished, Max excused himself briefly and returned with two bowls of fresh peach cobbler.

"Alex, what would you say if I told you that everything you're experiencing is absolutely normal for someone as talented and hardworking as you are?" Max asked almost apologetically.

"I'd say you were a pretty cruel person," Alex teased.

"It does sound cruel," Max admitted. "The truth is you've got a lot to be proud of. A majority of aspiring real estate agents and business owners would have quit long ago. But you haven't."

"In truth, you've done pretty well for yourself. So well, in fact, that you've reached a ceiling of achievement."

Alex gave Max an inquisitive look that invited him to further explain what he meant.

"Ceilings of achievement are a natural part of business," Max explained.

"You see Alex, your talent and hard work have taken you a long way. Because of this, you've been able to be fairly entrepreneurial with your business and still achieve a respectable level of success."

"However, talent and hard work can only take you so far. At some point natural law requires that you approach your business in a more purposeful way."

For the first time, Alex felt as though someone else truly understood his situation. What's more, there was something in his gut that told him Max might actually be able to help him.

"Max, that is exactly it," Alex responded. "I know that I need to become more purposeful, as you say it. In fact, I'm always trying to be more purposeful."

"The challenge is that as soon as I focus on one part of my business, I have problems because I neglect another part. Progress seems so slow. At my rate, it will take forever to break through my ceiling of achievement, as you say it."

"Well said," Max answered. "The secret is not just being purposeful, but how you approach being purposeful. The only way to truly accelerate your progress is to use a holistic approach that addresses all the key areas of your business simultaneously."

"Fifteen years ago I was in the same place you are now. I wasn't about to give up on my dream of being a successful restaurateur, but I knew I needed to make some big changes," Max began.

"Around the same time, a good friend of mine, who also happens to be a real estate agent, took part in a unique Challenge that introduced him to a special business formula that contained the type of holistic, purposeful approach we're talking about," Max continued.

"Not only did this formula make my friend wildly successful, but he also shared with me…in the form of a Challenge of course."

"Let me tell you, my business literally hasn't been the same since."

"In fact, Alex, this is the reason I was hoping to see you this evening. For some time now I've wanted to offer this same Challenge, the Freedom Challenge, to you."

Alex could hardly believe his ears. It felt so improbable that the answers that seemed so elusive just a few minutes ago might now be within his grasp.

"I've guided numerous people through the Freedom Challenge over the years," Max continued. "And I've grown quite good at it."

"However, I've got something special in mind for you. There's someone I'd like you to meet and, if he's willing, he'd be the perfect person to offer you the Challenge."

Without waiting for Alex to voice his approval, Max rose from his seat and disappeared as he crossed over to the other side of the crowded dining room.

Max returned within a few minutes with a well-dressed, distinguished looking gentleman whom Alex thought looked vaguely familiar.

"Alex Okamura, I'd like you to meet Chuck Stevens," said Max.

Again, Alex could hardly believe his ears. Chuck Stevens was a bona fide business legend in Reed County.

The local paper had just run a series of articles about Chuck Stevens revealing that, in addition to founding Villa Properties, one of the most successful real estate companies in the state, Chuck was also the head of an elite international venture capitalist group that provides financial backing to startup businesses in developing countries.

Rumor also had it that Chuck was considering running for U.S. Congress.

Recovering his composure, Alex calmly introduced himself, "It's my pleasure Mr. Stevens. Your reputation precedes you."

"Please, call me Chuck," Chuck responded. "Do you mind if I join you for a few minutes Alex?"

"Not at all," Alex answered.

"Alex, I'm going be direct," Chuck began. "You've got what it takes to be one of the top agents in Reed County and more. Not only do I hear great things about you from within the real estate community, but Max speaks quite highly of you as well."

"At the same time, you've reached a ceiling of achievement. One that is not easily broken. I know because I once faced the same one myself."

"Max shared with me that he's offered you the Freedom Challenge. If you'd have me as your coach, I'd be honored to show you how to break through your ceiling of achievement and take control of your business and life in a way you never thought possible."

"Will you accept the Freedom Challenge?" Chuck asked without hesitation.

By now Alex had overcome his disbelief and was slightly skeptical.

"What's the catch?" Alex responded.

I'm glad you asked," Chuck replied. "There are two requirements."

"First, you must keep a journal and write down everything from our coaching sessions and the all the meetings you have."

"Second, at some point in your career, you must share the Freedom Challenge with at least one other person."

With that, Chuck sat back in his chair and allowed Alex to make his decision just as Guy Chamberlain had done for him nearly two decades earlier.

"I accept," Alex finally said, breaking the silence.

"Great," said Chuck before Alex could analyze his decision further. "I'd like to get started right away. Can you meet me back here on Friday at 4 pm for our first coaching session?"

"Yes," answered Alex as he used his phone to check his calendar.

"Friday it is then," said Chuck. "I'll see you at 4 pm. Don't forget to bring your journal and be sure to dress comfortably. We won't spend much time indoors…"

# AUTHORS'
# NOTE TO
# THE READER

Thank you for making the investment in this book. Our goal was to provide you with a relatable overview of the documented strategies of the Fast Forward program, a revolutionary game designed to teach top agents how to master their real estate businesses and free themselves from the chaos that inevitably accompanies financial success.

While the ideas and concepts presented in this book stand solidly on their own merit, they become even more effective when combined with tactical instruction. A detailed description of the tactics associated with the Freedom Formula was outside the scope of this book, but there are several vehicles for learning more:

1.  Specialized, one-on-one coaching is available through Think Custom Coaching.

    (Visit www.thinkcustomcoaching.com to learn more)

2.  An eight week group coaching program that is tailored specifically for the Freedom Challenge is available through Think Custom Coaching which will guide you through the setup and first few weeks of playing your game.

    (Visit www.thinkcustomcoaching.com to learn more)

3.  The Fast Forward program, a self-paced, reality game that allows an agent to build his or her business while playing is available for purchase online.

    This easy-to-follow system includes over 7 hours of pre-recorded coaching and a 40 page field guide that details all the strategies referenced in Guy Chamberlain's Freedom Challenge.

    (Visit www.fastforwardgame.com to learn more)

Of course, you may discover or create your own vehicle of learning. Regardless, we couldn't be more excited about the journey on which you are about to embark. Here's to your 'Higher Purpose of Business'!

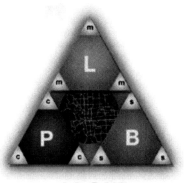

# ABOUT
# CHRIS ANGELL

After pursuing a Master's in Education, training for Starbucks, and selling real estate for over 6 years, Chris Angell became the CEO of a multi-million dollar real estate brokerage with over 200 agents.

Having taught audiences of all sizes across the country, Chris Angell now offers his insights through speaking, coaching and writing. Chris Angell is the founder of think Custom Coaching, a boutique coaching company for small businesses emphasizing systems, brand strategy and behavior specific lead generation strategies to name a few.

Chris lives in Washington State with his wife and two children.

# ABOUT
# CHRIS INVERSO

Chris Inverso is a small business author, speaker, and consultant. He holds an MBA from the University of Washington and has 15 years of combined real estate, franchising, and banking experience.

As a native of the Pacific Northwest, Chris resides in Tacoma, WA with his wife Tharen and their three daughters Siri, Elise, and Macy.

# YOUR JOURNAL

# YOUR JOURNAL

9 780615 500942